writers in the Spirit

Praise for *Writers in the Spirit*

"It has been said that most people, even those who say they want to write, do not actually want to write; they want to have written—a very different desire. Carol Rottman will help you move from merely wanting to write to actually writing. Her book is filled with insight, encouragement, and practical wisdom for writers and would-be writers."

Daniel Taylor, author of *Tell Me a Story* and
In Search of Sacred Places

"I have a lot of books on writing, but rarely come across one that turns my devotional time into a preparation for and inspiration to write. *Writers in the Spirit* helps connect me to God while reminding me that writing is a gift from Him and a calling to be both treasured and nurtured."

Sally E. Stuart
Christian Writers' Market Guide

I am grateful for the appearance of *Writers in the Spirit*, an eclectic conjoining of memoir and devotional along with advice to writers and helpful observations from many talented writers. Rottman's book looks at the writing life through the prism of faith, a fertile territory for the plow.

W. Dale Brown
Professor of English
Director, Festival of Faith & Writing
Calvin College

"I thank Carol Rottman for sharing her journey with me. Her inspiration for others comes, in part, from the accounting of her own struggles to be in the mode of becoming the writer; her reflections on her own values, faith commitment, relationships, and struggles with the issues of life and meaning. I could identify with much of what she has experienced, at times with a smile and at other times with a throb of the heart. I am happy to recommend it to aspiring writers, who, like Carol, want to develop and use their "god-like" gift."

Rev. Peter Borgdorff
Executive Director of Ministries
The Christian Reformed Church in North America

"Carol Rottman is a widely read, thoughtful Christian who takes joy not only in her own writing, but particularly in encouraging and helping along other Christians who themselves would like to write. She has demonstrated her ability to help aspiring amateur writers by very successfully teaching a number of courses in this area for the Calvin Academy for Life-long Learning, which is affiliated with Calvin College. Her grateful students have appreciated in particular both the skills she has taught them and her affirming, non-threatening attitude toward them. Nor does she teach them mere skills for their own sake; a life lived deeply has taught her the inestimable value and richness of clear and winsome writing "in the Spirit." With this practical, inspiring volume, that includes essays, meditations, and down-to-earth advice, she invites a wider audience to share her insights and joy in that venture."

Dr. Wallace Bratt, Director of Curriculum
for Calvin Academy for Life-long Learning and
Emeritus Professor of Germanic Languages, Calvin College

"This is as much a book for pastors as it is for writers. Most pastors would benefit from following Rottman's advice 'to resist the temptation to tack on the gospel at the end,' but rather 'subtly infuse the whole piece with good news.' With Carol Rottman, I urge writers to accept God's gift with joy—explore it, experiment with it, and 'Rejoice in the Lord always,' as you use the gift entrusted to you."

Rev. Arthur Schoonveld
Retired Pastor
The Christian Reformed Church in North America

"*Writers in the Spirit* is a gift from one writer to another. In this book Carol Rottman presents devotions, tips, and challenges to fellow Christian writers. From her own experience, she humbly offers advice and understanding along the way, knowing both the exhilaration and the exhaustion of being a writer. This book will encourage those who, like Carol, walk with the Spirit and record that journey with words."

Rev. Kathleen Smith, Director of Continuing Education
Calvin Institute of Christian Worship and
Calvin Theological Seminary

Inspiration
for
Christian
Writers

writers in the Spirit

Carol J. Rottman, Ph.D.

FaithWalk
PUBLISHING
Grand Haven, Michigan

Published by FaithWalk Publishing
Grand Haven, Michigan 49417

Scripture quotations, unless otherwise indicated, are taken from the HOLY BIBLE, NEW INTERNATIONAL VERSION®. NIV®. Copyright ©1973, 1978, 1984 by International Bible Society. Used by permission of Zondervan. All rights reserved.

Printed in the United States of America

09 08 07 06 05 04   7 6 5 4 3 2 1

Library of Congress Cataloging-in Publication Data

Rottman, Carol J.
 Writers in the Spirit : inspiration for Christian writers / by Carol Rottman.
   p. cm.
 ISBN 1-932902-43-0 (pbk. : alk. paper)
 1. Christian literature—Authorship. I. Title.
 PN3377.5.C47R68 2004
 808'.06623—dc22

                          2004011359

Dedication

In memory of my mother,
Casey Vanden Bosch (1911–2004),
mentor, model for living, and friend.

Acknowledgments

I am honored that God put many people into my life to inspire me as a writer. In addition to the myriad of authors whose books I have devoured, there are teachers: Richard Tiemersma, Howard Goldstein, Jenny Clark, Linda Tuthill, Mark Hiskes, and Cecile Goding. I give special thanks to Veralyn Koops Davids for challenging me to write this book, Lois Roelofs, a fellow-writer and on-line consultant, and Mary Zwaanstra, sister and confidant.

Graditude goes also to writers who honed first drafts: Grand Rapids Writers' Group; Grandville Creative Christian Writers; Iowa workshop participants; and present and former students. I hold a deep appreciation for Louann Werksma, Ginny McFadden, and Dirk Wierenga at FaithWalk Publishing who artfully carried this book to completion.

To my family, all artists in their own right, I offer the last words—for pushing, coaching, and leaving me alone—so I could write: my children, Barbara, Douglas, and Susan, and their families; my late parents, Marvin and Casey; and especially, my loyal husband and encourager, Fritz.

Preface

I gave a copy of a favorite book, Susan Shaughnessy's *Walking on Alligators: A Book of Meditations for Writers*,[1] to a friend after a rare reunion in California, the spring of 2001. We grew up together in South Denver and share not only a birthday but also a passion for writing. In the book I penned a disclaimer, "Enjoy this purely secular book, meant to motivate the reluctant writer." Later she thanked me—with a challenge: "Why don't you write a similar book for writers who are Christians?"

Her suggestion has haunted me like some unholy ghost. Much as I wanted, I couldn't get the idea to go away. I reread *Alligators* and realized again its importance to me. When doubts about writing, complacency, and inertia get the best of me, I need a push. Not from a bully or an authority, but by a fellow struggler. In the same way that Anne Lamott's *Bird by Bird*[2] takes every writerly excuse and turns it upside down, Shaughnessy identifies with my daily doubts. She meditates on words of other writers in ways that reveal her own trials and self doubts. They mirror my own. Even her most profound insights are honestly submitted to us with an offhand ring of self-revelation.

Part of my difficulty, and perhaps your own, has to do with God's claim on my life and work. I recently retired from paid work in order to write. But how do I find the motivation I need every day, as I face the blank page? How can I justify spending so much time writing without clear knowledge of the usefulness or worth of my work? While Rome burns, will I just fiddle with my words? And then the big question: Is this really what God wants me to do with my life?

This book records the thoughts of one called (if only by a faithful friend) to tackle a job she had not previously envisioned. I testify to a mysterious leading by God's Spirit. Using Bible passages and quotations from writers who are also Christian, I remain in awe, as in the words of an old hymn, of being "filled with messages from Thee."

Several years ago, I traveled to hear Frederick Buechner speak the words I had read over and over:

> *Listen to your life.*
> *See it for the fathomless mystery that it is.*
> *In the boredom and pain of it no less than in the*
> *excitement and gladness; touch, taste, smell your way to the*
> *holy and hidden heart of it because in the last analysis*
> *all moments are key moments, and life itself is grace.*[3]

In his humble, heartfelt way, he convinced me. Nothing great or small is beyond pondering as a moment of grace.

In that spirit, I offer these meditations and personal essays to other writers who profess God's lordship over their vocation. We travel the same unmarked road, day by day, led by the Spirit.

Carol J. Rottman
Greenville, Michigan

Contents

Introduction

"And the Word became flesh and made his dewlling among us," living in our houses and our studies, at our desks or café tables—even in our hearts and minds.

Recently a pastor asked those assembled at a wedding ceremony to puzzle with her why God called Jesus "the Word" at his incarnation. Why not "love" or "truth" or "grace" as Jesus is called in various places in Scripture? The pastor speculated that God trusted the power of words to reveal himself, just as the new bride and groom used their vows to reveal themselves and their intentions to the other. The couple wrote the words before they spoke them, an act that stresses the lifelong impact of vows carefully chosen. Words spoken are remembered for a while, but words written last much longer.

Writers in the Spirit honors written words and those who write them. God's Word and Spirit led me to speculate on human words and what it takes to select, record, and create meaning through them. I also share selected wisdom from other writers who have written about writing. This book encourages the reader to explore various aspects of writing by means of short meditations and longer essays grouped under inspirational themes. The text aims to guide instead of prescribe. There is no magic formula to good writing; each new or experienced writer must find his or her own way.

Writers in the Spirit is one Christian writer's attempt to encourage other Christians who write to join in the fascinating and freeing vocation of writing. Each of us has in some way felt God's call to use words as our medium of expression. That call is less a command than an invitation into a whole new way of life. Many writers testify to finding more joy in the act of writing than in the final product. As Philip Yancey once said "As a writer, I play with words all day. I toy with them, listen for their overtones, crack them open, and try to stuff my thoughts inside."[4]

This book also seeks to inspire the reluctant or "sometime" writer to continue to write. Lest you consider stopping short of application, there are tips and tools to aid you in active writing. The hints are a compilation of ideas of other writers that have proven useful over the years to me as a writer and to the students in writing workshops and classes I've taught. They are practical suggestions meant to move you from the comfort of thought to the exhilaration of action.

The end of each chapter contains a writing challenge. Merely thinking about writing will not produce a single word. Endless speculation may actually block writing instead of promoting it. Each assignment has the potential to convince you to take up your pen and write. Some of us don't really know what we are thinking until we write it.

The success of this book to inspire and encourage depends on your tangible response—words on the page. Some may use it as a daily meditation before the day's writing begins. Others will take the writing challenge and create stories in the privacy of their own home. Or you may choose to use it as a text for a writers' group and together work through the book, including its assignments, ultimately sharing and critiquing each other's work. Perhaps others will make of this book a gift to friends who are hesitant writers, and in so doing instill in them the confidence to do what they have only dreamed.

With God's Word and Spirit as our guides, all of us can become writers in the Spirit.

Incarnational

Many atheists deny God because they care so passionately about a caring and personal God, and the world around them is inconsistent with a God of love, they feel, and so they say, "There is no God."

But even when one denies God, to serve music, or painting, or words is a religious activity, whether or not the conscious mind is willing to accept the fact. Basically there can be no categories such as "religious" art and "secular" art, because all true art is incarnational, and therefore, "religious."

Madeleine L'Engle[1]

1

"A nd the Word became flesh" may be the ultimate mystery of God. At a moment in human history, God changed from spirit to flesh. An idea *of* the divine became an experience *with* the person of God. People saw, touched, heard, and even felt Christ's presence through wedding wine, bread for the masses, and the hem of a robe.

All art, says Madeleine L'Engle, shares that mysterious spirit-to-flesh transformation. Art is incarnational. The song or the poem or the sketch enfleshes an idea and brings it within human reach. Words or images give life to stray ideas. They leave a map not unlike the trail of crumbs Hansel and Gretel dropped to help them find their way home. All artists yearn to use created matter and mold it into a comprehensible form.

"Incarnate" is a better word for what artists do than "create." They make something out of other somethings; they are the great recyclers of this world. There may not be anything "new" under the sun, but wordsmiths—as well as carvers, painters, composers, and inventors—will forever strive to reshape the clay of their own experience into objects of beauty and truth.

A Double Portion

When they had crossed, Elijah said to Elisha, "Tell me, what can I do for you before I am taken from you?" "Let me inherit a double portion of your spirit," Elisha replied.

II Kings 2:9

Years before my mother died, I overheard her tell a friend she wished the Lord would take her like he took Elijah—on a whirlwind in a chariot—without dying. For people of her age, the fear of the dying process far exceeds the fear of death itself. My father probably had the same fears, but he died in his sleep, quickly—and, we assume, painlessly. That would be Mom's second choice of a way to go.

Elijah had been told in advance that he would be "taken up." He was on his way to meet God along with Elisha, his friend and successor, via Gilgal and Bethel and Jericho and the Jordan. At each stop the old man urged the younger one to go back, while resident prophets reminded Elisha that his mentor would be "taken today." Elisha vowed not to leave. Finally Elijah asked pointedly what Elisha wanted from him before leaving. Elisha didn't hesitate: "Your spirit, doubled."

For my father and Elijah, leaving suddenly was a blessing, but for the Elishas among us, it is torturous. We are looking for a word or, even more, a blessing from our mentors. We have happily followed, but the leader is now going where we cannot follow. Ready or not, the leader's job passes to us.

When my pastor preached on this text, she reminded me that the double portion is what the eldest son inherited. Elisha didn't ask for more goods or property—just for more of his mentor's spirit.

Even though he and I never acknowledged that relationship, my father was my writing mentor. He was not an overt teacher. His influence was far more subtle—much of it dawning on me slowly during the twenty years since his passing. But if I had had a warning of his being taken from this earth, I, like Elisha, would have begged for his "spirit blessing," even as his second-born daughter.

Elisha received a symbol of his mentor's blessing—a cloak. "Carry on God's work," the hair shirt must have reminded him. I have such a symbol: letters and journals and memoirs, a bundle of writing from my father's hand. These words I treasure as my "double portion."

Dear God,

As we were taught, let us teach others with encouragement and an infectious spirit. Amen.

Meditation Mornings

I will meditate on all your works and consider all your mighty deeds.

Psalm 77:12

Read Scripture, pray, write—five minutes each. A great way to start the day, I thought, when my husband and I were spending a sabbatical year in Boulder, Colorado. His work took him and our only car away early and all day, and I continued my freelance technical writing from a makeshift desk in our small apartment. Spartan living to be sure, but less filled with distractions than usual. Involvement with friends and church no longer filled nights and weekends. In this setting, I began the daily practice of meditation.

The first Sunday in our temporary church home, someone offered me a Lenten meditation guide—a small booklet with a text and a thought to complete each day. The setting was perfectly quiet, without distractions, and I was open in ways the press of living sometimes prevents. Soon the blank book became the focal point of each day, and a pattern was established.

How did this happen? I hate routine. I have always felt that days should have their own flavor, not the sameness of the day before. Even devotions, as we always called daily Bible reading, can dull us. But this was different: I was asked to record thoughts the passage brought to mind. Finally I penned down my free-floating half-thoughts. Later, when I read the pages, it was as if for the first time.

My husband faithfully reads a chapter in his Bible before going to sleep, while I'm into *The Atlantic* or *Writers' Digest*. He never wants to talk about what he's read at that time of night. He doesn't feel the need to "do something" with a passage or a verse or a word. He may have a better picture of God's redemption story, but I need to deal with each little picture. While reading, my pen must be in my hand and an open page before me.

Boulder was a center for meditation—very little of it on Scripture. Our next door neighbor led seminars on "Mountain Path Meditation" propelled by the god within. My starting point will always be the Word. By my plodding method I will never read the whole book many times as is true for my routine-loving husband. But I do have something to show for "read, pray, write"—many pages of inspired writing. This kind of reading launched a dialogue of thought, prayer, and listening for God's voice.

My African-American friends like to talk about "being in the Word." Meditation keeps me in that place where wisdom waits. Whether my text is chosen at random or comes from the Common Lectionary or a favorite book of the Bible, it captures my heart and won't let me go until I think about it deeply. And taking all the time I need, then make a record …

Spirit of God,
"Every time I feel the Spirit moving in my heart, I pray …" Thank you for making each day new. Amen.

It's Only a Game

W e were not a game family. No one sat long enough empty-handed to wonder what could fill the hours. Competition among us, the five siblings, and between our parents, took subtle forms not half as civilized as a game of Yahtzee or Canasta or Clue. Puzzles better suited our individualistic ways. But when I was fourteen, we bought an old house in a deserted mining town in Colorado, where Dad determined we would spend a month every summer, far away from Denver and his busy medical practice. In the ancient clapboard house without electricity, running water, or indoor facilities we tested our skills of self-reliance and made an attempt to unite as a family, perhaps to learn to play together.

The kerosene lamps were not quite bright enough for reading at night, but they showed the Scrabble board and the small wooden tiles just fine. Dad not only picked the game; he dictated and enforced the rules. He prided himself in word usage, meaning, and especially pronunciation. There was never a word we laid on the anagram-style board that he did not know. An avid crossword puzzler, Mom knew odd words, many of them small enough to fit when places to attach letters were few. My older sister Mary was quick and verbal; I, on the other hand, was slow and ponderous and needed help with my spelling. The younger kids watched, hoping at least to read the words laid on the board.

Scrabble moves slowly, especially for a fierce competitor like my father. He wasn't satisfied with any word; he needed the best word. Demanding patience and absolute silence from the crowd while he was thinking, he finally snapped down the tiles with authority. Between turns, he made sure the tiles already played were neatly placed within their lines on the board and the score was accurate. The game was not fun; it was war, and he was the commander-in-chief. Woe to anyone who would challenge a word that Dad laid—he would grab the beat-up dictionary and prove them wrong. During games of Scrabble, I suddenly realized that being a doctor was not the skill he valued most. Dear to

Dad's heart were the words and thought and reason of one schooled in classical literature.

In the early 1930s, before science classes dominated a would-be doctor's course of study, he soaked up the great books and wrote freely. Many years later when I attended his alma mater, I searched (on a tip from Mom) the old Calvin College *Chimes*[2] for Dad's poetry published under the assumed name "Carter." Apparently he was unwilling to identify himself alongside the likes of Peter DeVries[3] and Feike Feikema[4]. When the competition thinned—as with his family over a game of Scrabble—he had no such hesitation. He was always the undisputed winner in the word war. We couldn't compete, even though we gave it our all.

Life within our household resembled the game of Scrabble. As in the game, Dad took command whenever he was home. Meals were unusually quiet for a family with five children. Dad prayed aloud before meals and read a Psalm afterward in his flawless diction and smooth baritone voice. There may have been chatter among us kids, but rarely conversation with our parents. Occasionally Dad would hold forth with a lecture—usually about some interesting medical case. It turned our stomachs; we couldn't wait to be excused. He always retired to his study after dinner.

The Great Depression that my father's generation endured, followed by the uncertainties of war, colored our family. Life was not intended to be fun, it was hard work. I hated holidays, for when my neighbor-friends were on outings to the mountains, we were home all day doing yard work. It was as if someone else had written the script but we just played the part. In that way we, and many in our close-knit Dutch-American community, shared a similar discomfort with leisure and just plain fun.

Even though Dad played some volleyball during the years he spent in the Army Air Force, he was not athletic. None of us was active in sports, unless you count my cheerleading foray (the only sport open to women at the time) and my eventual competitive running. Subtle messages conveyed that playing sports for fun was a waste of time. I recall Dad's comment after he attended his one and only basketball game: "It's a good place to forget your troubles; you can't think with all that noise."

Mind games like Scrabble, with their calculated moves, mirrored our family interactions. I often wondered what Dad was thinking, as I did during the board games. He was careful not to show his hand until all the kinks were worked out; it was a pronouncement not to be challenged.

The old post-Depression ideal of the "self-made man" seemed to be Dad's goal. Outside the family he was like one of those new Scrabble boards with the little ridges around the letter squares that keep the pieces from sliding out of place. In the community he was known as a visionary, a compassionate obstetrical doctor, a fixture on committees of church and Christian school, and a generous giver. Within the family, and to his children, he remained a mystery.

When I married and left home, I put aside the game of Scrabble except for a few rare times in the mountain cabin while staying with my extended family. My husband joined the game only once. When no one would adopt his proposed time-limit-per-turn, he lost patience. We, with our children, never became a game family.

When my Dad died in his sleep at age seventy, I knew it was a fitting end to his game. He worked until the day he died. But in the end he left to my siblings and me his prized possession—words on paper—one hundred pages of memoir! I am convinced that any ability I have in writing came through his genes, not through his teaching. Unless, of course, I count the slow, deliberate, thoughtful effort I learned playing Scrabble with him: to find just the right word, put it down on paper, and win the game.

Tips, Hints, and Advice

Carefully choose a place to write, a time to write, and materials for the task.

1. You would not be reading this book if it weren't for a stirring within urging you to write. The impetus may seem almost biological—a gift from the past via genetic transmission—and, therefore, not clearly understood. Most of the world does not feel the pressure you do to put your thoughts and stories on paper. Give your desire a voice; spell it out.

2. You've been told you have a flair for writing. Someone saw an article you wrote for your church newsletter and complimented you. Ask yourself if the process of writing gave you pleasure or pain. If the latter is true you may brush off the compliment and never volunteer again. But if pleasure, or at least satisfaction, comes whenever you create with words, assign yourself another article, just for fun.

3. My first assignment for every new creative writing class has three parts: Carefully choose a place to write, a time to write, and materials for the task. The place includes a room, a writing surface, and a chair. The time you choose may be the same time each day or a week's allotment for writing, squeezed into several slots in a busy schedule. The materials can range from pen, paper, and pencil to a laptop or desk computer. Since I draft in longhand, the pen and paper must be exquisitely compatible. Make the choices that suit *you* best. They are the tools of your trade; their quality and "fit" will make a difference in your writing life.

4. I always knew when the preacher had come to the end of the sermon: "Let us …" or "Go ye

and …" or "Pray without ceasing." A simple declarative sentence pointing at me as one of the "us" or the "ye" or the understood "you." If your story rests on the last sermonic point, it has failed. Resist the temptation to tack on the gospel at the end. Subtly infuse the whole piece with "good news."

**Writing
Challenge**

1

*Write about
a person
who has
mentored you.*

As you begin or continue your journey into writing, think of a person, like I have of my father, who mentored you in the past or is mentoring you today. Not all mentors are positive encouragers. Some mentors are unaware that you look to them for courage to go on. Scrabble, the one game we played as a family, gave me keen interest in words. The value my father placed on them—the sound of proper pronunciation, their usefulness in anagram competition, and the amazing way they carry meaning—surprised me then and astounds me now.

Write about a person who has mentored or is mentoring you. Tell your story, with as much color, detail, and honesty as befits the love of the written word, which the two of you share. Place your tale in time and space. Bring the relationship to life, put flesh on your ideas.

Nourishment

2

The lake in front of my home was noticeably low this fall until four days of rain poured in or seeped through the ground into it. Once again the lake's plant life, fish, and waterfowl will find what they need to survive the winter and bring forth new life in the spring. Nature is feeding this lake.

I have not been feeding the lake that Jean Rhys mentions. The activity of long summer days as well as the lure of the out-of-doors has its effects on my writing. Writing alone, without a quota for output, my trickle of words is in danger of drying up. But winter is coming. I will not bemoan its sunless skies or its icy roads. They will keep me in a good place—at my desk—without distraction, being nourished by the living water of the Spirit, until my cup overflows on the page.

In My Own Words

I assure you before God that what I am writing you is no lie.

Galatians 1:20

I watched the scene on the screen with horror: German soldiers forcing the Frank family and friends to pack in five minutes before herding them away to an unknown fate. Anne grabs things, considers her diary and her stories but lets them fall, scattering, onto the floor. "Her diary!" I wail. "Why doesn't she take her diary?" As the hideaways are forced from their annex shelter, Meep, their Gentile protector, rushes upstairs to rescue valuables left behind before the Nazis return. She frantically gathers the papers, rushes downstairs, and dumps them into an office drawer.

I had the same powerful response while watching *Dances with Wolves*[2] and saw John Dunbar's journal floating in the pond. "Not his diary! Save it!" Even fictional characters deserve to survive through their words.

The new TV adaptation of *The Diary of Anne Frank*[3] continues through the unimaginable concentration camp confinement and death. Knowing the end of the story doesn't ease my pain, but seeing Anne's writing, still in the drawer, gives the story its triumph. Anne's words survived!

Not all of us write immortal words—and certainly not at age fourteen. At a fortieth high school class reunion I met an old friend, now living in California. "I think I still have a story you wrote in high school. I'll see if I can dig it up," she said. Months later she sent the yellowed steno-pad sheets containing my adolescent romance story, in my own hand. My story will not change how we look at history—I am no Anne Frank. But by indirect means even my forgotten story survived.

For some of us, who we are—the real self—comes out in words written raw—not the final draft edited for the reader, but the first words from the heart. My personal journals of the past twenty years are beginning to fill a shelf in my study. Now they are for my eyes only, but I've already designated a keeper of my journals for a time when there will be no secrets worth keeping. I always wished that my grandmothers, whom I never knew because they died before I was born, had left some written record. Many times I have longed to know my foremothers. Perhaps a great, great grandchild will, someday, find my words and know me.

Dear God,

    Thank you for blank books and pens and computers to record my words. Preserve the written word, each generation's testimony to your faithfulness. Amen.

Don't Call—Write

I, Paul, write this greeting in my own hand. Remember my chains. Grace be with you.

Colossians 4:18

No wonder the U.S. Postal Service is going broke. If it weren't for magazines and junk mail, my mailbox would be empty. But every day I walk the quarter-mile driveway to the roadside box in happy anticipation. Maybe this will be the day. But no. My most recent letter arrived a week before from a sister in Colorado. It was a treasure—I handled it often, just looking at the postmark and the extra stamps to cover its bulk, and read it many times before announcing to my husband the big news: "We got a *letter* from Sue!" Sue writes because she doesn't do e-mail, but her kind are an endangered species.

This week I handled a sheaf of letters from my father, written over a period of ten years, most with personal notes handwritten on the back of the photocopied one. Absolutely amazing! For a decade my father had a traveling job as a hospital accreditor. He and my mother traveled by truck, towing an Airstream trailer, from state to state. They parked the trailer in a central location, and Dad went to work from there. The nomadic life was surprisingly pleasant for both of them. Dad decided he would keep in touch by writing a weekly letter, duplicating it for the five children and his siblings. He collected our return letters at hospitals we selected from a list he had sent us of his planned stops.

My sister Sue and I talk about letters. Her children live away from her, too, and they are never out of touch—by phone.

"But calls don't leave a permanent record!" she wails. Nor do e-mail messages, unless the recipient feels they are significant enough to print and save. This was true of my brother, who met a woman through letters on the Internet. That relationship led to an on-line courtship. At their wedding, four 3-inch binders were on display filled with their "love letters."

Recently I was reminded that St. Paul would never have written the letters to the churches if he had not been incarcerated and unable to preach. Writing was his substitute method of getting out God's word; and we, thousands of years later, still faithfully read his letters. We have no idea what he said in his sermons.

Do I have a complicated message, a story, a testimony I want to say just right? I'll start with letters—they could be my first book!

Dear God,

You used the simple letter to give us your truth as well as your demonstration of love. We are blessed daily by your words. Amen.

Memoir and Memory

Whoever knows what you're thinking and planning except you yourself? The same with God.

I Corinthians 2:11, *The Message*

R eading memoir is my passion. Give me real life over fiction any day. Because good memoir is also that of "the examined life," it has advantages over biography, which is firmly grounded in history and recorded documents. It is secondhand. The historical novel gives license to speculate on the mind of a person, but the imagination of the writer colors the story with shades he selects. Even autobiography, which often seems limited to famous persons who have an ax to grind or a spicy story to uncover, seems less insightful than memoir.

But memoir—those odd bits of memory that are isolated and then examined—ring true to real life for me. I see my own life in snippets of another person's closer look at his own. I'm reading a good one this week: *Chasing the Hawk*, by Andrew Sheehan[4]; he is the son of Dr. George Sheehan, whose philosophy in *Running and Being*[5] had a profound effect on me in the 1970s when I took his advice and started running. It is a son's story about coming of age alongside a famous father. I can't leave the book alone; its magnetism for me comes from its parallels with my own life. The setting and the situations are certainly different—Andrew was one of twelve children in a Catholic family—but the emotional insights are captivating. In some passages I can imagine the author speaking with my voice, putting into words things I have not yet said. His examined life becomes my chance to delve into the recesses of my own.

But just one memoir cannot do for me. I am insatiable. There are so many facets of my past and present, which have nothing to do with the father/daughter dynamics. So I devour Kathleen Norris's[6] writing about places of the heart, Patricia Hampl's[7] search to understand her strict Catholic upbringing, and John Hockenberry's[8] and Nancy Mairs'[9] and André Dubus's[10] quest for a full life from the seat of a wheelchair.

My own memoir falls out in fits and starts, thematic little essays and meditations—each one a fragment of a complex existence. I am reminded that I'm one more trickle, to quote Jean Rhys, just "feeding the lake." I wasn't asked to fill it; just to keep it and myself from going dry.

Spirit of God,
Help me understand my own thoughts. Reveal yourself to me as I work.
Amen.

Memoirs of Grace

A writing of Hezekiah king of Judah after his illness and recovery: I said, "In the prime of my life must I go through the gates of death and be robbed of the rest of my years?"

Isaiah 38: 9,10

In Isaiah we read the story of King Hezekiah, who was near death because of an apparent infection caused by a festering boil. After God promised recovery and fifteen more years, Hezekiah wrote the story of his struggle with God, which he describes: "Like a weaver I have rolled up my life, and he has cut me off from the loom." He reminded God, "The living, the living—they praise you as I am doing today; fathers tell their children about your faithfulness."[11]

Many of us write while recovering from illness or enduring grave trials. My father had his first heart attack when he was in his prime. In those days doctors prescribed mandatory rest for at least two months. He had never rested in his life. As a way to cheer him, my sister suggested he write the story of his interesting life. So he began his autobiography on lined yellow legal pads as he sat in the wide-armed chair with his feet propped on the footstool. He was always a facile writer, so even in his forced resting stage he became productive in a new way.

None of us saw his writing until after his last fatal attack, some fifteen years later. His autobiography was filled with meticulous detail—especially of his years in medical school. He dedicated the book to the daughter who prompted him to write. Mom fulfilled his instructions and typed his handwritten words into nearly one hundred pages of memoir for his five children and his surviving siblings.

When his children had read the book, we shared our reactions. The writing was beautiful; his clarity of thought astounding. But we were sad. For all its detail, the memoir lacked the specifics we most craved—loving remembrances of us. In contrast to Hezekiah's book, there was even more missing—a reminder of God's faithfulness. A memoir can be a message to the next generation. I ask myself today, "Which of my stories will tell about God's abiding presence in my life?" Events without reflection are only history. With reflection, they can also be testimony.

Dear God,

You have been my faithful God. May my writing capture your living presence in all the events of my life. Amen.

Hiking through Suburbia

*T**hese boots were made for walking.*" I hum absently as I hunt for the faded blue-hooded sweatshirt and pull on the old hiking boots. Not very fancy duds in this upscale neighborhood, but I dress for comfort, which means baggy and well worn. As I slip out of the front door and make my way to the road, a nippy autumn breeze catches me short, and my eyes respond with spontaneous tears. This is my favorite season, always full of bright surprises.

The ample front lawns that border the boulevard have no sidewalks, so I must share the two-lane road with dozens of speeding cars as I walk on the left, facing traffic. The median that separates the one-way lanes of Gates Mills Boulevard is broad, but the terrain is uneven and, after abundant rain, soggy. My boots are used to a lively pace, so I too hit the asphalt and take a defensive stance toward the mechanical enemies. I sense that hasty commuters would chance hitting me rather than pause to change lanes and give me a safe space. So I remain ready to leap on the grassy border and roll if necessary while I navigate the thoroughfare toward the nearest side street. I am aware not only of vehicular danger in my path along the curb, but of all other impediments as well—the road kill, the flattened cans, the puddle that may have turned to ice overnight.

At last I turn off the main street to a road curving down a hill, trading exhaust fumes for the scent of dew on newly cut grass. My body moves rhythmically, like a well oiled engine. With the whir of traffic fading, I begin to hear the creatures of the woods: the sassy raven, the tree squirrel, the dove mewing on the wires overhead. I try to get in tune. My boots are nearly noiseless, and I hope to see the herd of young deer that come to water in the gully. I cannot see them today, but I sense they may be watching me from just inside the thicket.

Soon my road path meets another, and I follow the loop to the left and begin the gradual climb up a longer street. My body labors and steams inside the sweatshirt I thought I needed to keep out the cold. Breathing deepens, and I feel my heart's beat joining in the musical motion of swinging arms and legs. About halfway up the hill, I reach a kind of reverie, my inside voice crowding out thoughts about the world around. Today I recall being in Colorado on a narrow mountain road, hiking many hours and miles, surrounded by cliffs that rise dramatically alongside a noisy stream. I smile at the eccentricity of devoting a whole day each summer to make my solo hike to Crystal City and back to Marble, a fifteen-mile loop from our mountain cabin. Suddenly a stone from the blacktop catches my shoe, and I feel I am really on that dusty Jeep road, climbing with my knapsack of lunch and notebook. I prefer the wild berries and itchweed of that landscape to the manicured hedges that line this street I walk today.

On today's two-mile hike I do not stop to take in the scenery or to make a journal entry, but I carry my treasures of memory and emotion around the block. I begin to think about the piece I've been asked to write for my high school class reunion. Memories rush in of the streets and roadways of South Denver, experienced on foot. I hear my mom's voice behind me as we walk to church, "Stand up straight, Carol; be glad you're tall." A few years later, walking tall with my high school books held inside a crooked arm, I travel from my home past small shops and through the Denver University campus, trying to mingle with the coeds. Today, I play with words that can describe my love of the hike, of pretending to be someone I'm not, of my moving body. Will those words come out in poetry or song because they were born in motion?

Two women appear at the top of the hill where the route bends again. They are marching in step with exaggerated arm motions, surely part of a fitness program. They hardly glance my way as they breeze past, looking smart in their bright walking outfits and filling the air with chatter. Their momentary presence interrupts my meditative state, reminding me that I walk to be alone, free from people noise. I care little whether hiking is good for my body; my body has always been good for the hike. Not only were these boots made for walking—*I* was made for walking.

Today's early morning trek renews me, even as spinning leaves remind me that soon the shorter days will keep me off the roadways at this hour. Never fear, there will be many more good times and places to walk, I reassure myself. On another day, perhaps with snow falling instead of leaves, I may jump up from my desk, in the middle of a sentence that isn't working, head out the door, and walk it out. Last week, the news of my daughter's miscarriage propelled me to the woods at midday. Some days I can't trust myself to see anything but erratic light through my tears, until I stumble along the path long enough to imagine some vision of the future.

My meandering mind is caught short when I come off the side street to the final stretch of boulevard that stands between my distant front door and me. The commuter traffic has thinned, replaced by the hazards of big cars driven by little old people who don't see me until they are almost upon me. I soften my disdain but I stay prepared to jump if necessary. The last leg of the hike brings me back to mental terra firma, forcing decisions about priorities for my day at work. My legs, now on autopilot, seem to swim on land effortlessly. They and I want to continue around another block for miles and miles and miles, but there is work to do. We obediently enter the door, shed the boots and outer shirt, and head to the kitchen for a hot cup of tea and a new day of writing.

**Tips,
Hints,
and
Advice**

*Writing is
like eating—
you need to
do it every
day or risk
starvation.*

1. When Jean Rhys tells writers to "feed the lake," she is referring to the body of written word collected over the ages. In order to feed that growing body, a writer must feed the source within him or herself. Reading, doing writing practice, journaling, cavorting with other writers can be bread for the writer. Keep eating even as you begin feeding the lake with your first published words.

2. Writing is also much like eating—you need to do it every day or risk starvation. Depending on your appetite and eating style, the sessions can be of the banquet or fast-food variety. If you miss too many meals, nourishment cannot happen. So write regularly—everyday if possible—and you will grow strong on the page. I don't work on Sunday; that's the day I write a letter home.

3. Letters to a friend or relative over time can become a permanent record of your life, a chronicle of the seasons and stages. If you type them on a computer, save them to a disk or print a copy. Even letters written in longhand can be photocopied and stored with your correspondent's reply. Substantial letters by e-mail can be stored or printed. I met a new friend at a writer's conference one summer, and a lively correspondence ensued, mostly about the passion we share for writing. Our friendship and our letter file are growing as well as valued critique of each other's work.

4. "Writer in Search of a Subject" might be the caption over most new writers' desks. So I should write everyday, you say, but what about? I've

heard conflicting advice: Write what you know; write what you don't know to find out about it; write your passions; write about everyday life. All are good advice. But for starters try these: Choose a character and follow him through a day; make a list of your obsessions and write about a strange one; pick two words at random and force them to be related. Exploring a subject is never a waste of time. Avoid thinking about its worth or usefulness while writing—that will come clear as you get your thoughts down.

5. Two things help me get unstuck when the writing stalls: Taking a power nap (putting my head on my folded arms at the desk until they tingle) or taking a walk. By letting go of the pen, ideas have a chance to germinate while the mind is at ease. Two things don't help: eating and fretting.

6. One of my writing heroes is the late Lewis B. Smedes.[12] My husband and I took a course from him in college and were overwhelmed by his breadth of theological knowledge. Brilliant but obscure, we thought at the time. What a delight to read, over the years, his very accessible books for everyday Christians. The more you know, the harder it is to speak with powerful simplicity. Smedes did just that. Many have learned practical Christianity from his works. Can you take a complex subject and make it understandable in a few words? That is a gift.

Writing Challenge

Look into your memory and find a person, place, or event to write about.

Words on paper last longer than thoughts. You or people who come after you can revisit recorded words. Stories can feed you; stories will feed the lake. What keeps your writer's well primed? Reading? Journaling? Running or walking? Letters? All seem to be attempts to capture the snippets of memory racing around in your head—memories too precious to let go.

Today's challenge is to direct your memory to a specific place and time. Close your eyes and return to the place of your *first* memory. Walk around that place with your eyes open. Go into your house and walk through it to the room where you slept. Now go outside into the yard or the field; then take a walk around the block or the back forty. Pull in names of people who live in houses or farms nearby. Recall streets, sidewalks, or lanes that lead to places you knew.

Walk around in your neighborhood until some image or person or event becomes too strong to push aside. *Write about it.* Fill in the details. Why won't this image, in particular, let you rest?

Understanding

Artists have always been drawn to the wild, wide elements they cannot control or understand—the sea, mountains, fire. To be an artist means to approach the light, and that means to let go our control, to allow our whole selves to be placed with absolute faith in that which is greater than we are. The novel we sit down to write and the one we end up writing may be very different, just as the Jesus we grasp and the Jesus who grasps us may also differ.

Madeleine L'Engle[1]

3

There is very little we know *for sure*. Even the truths we hold of God's creation, our fall and redemption, are claimed by faith, not proof. The artist's search for understanding among the wild and uncontrollable elements of nature will not yield absolute truth. Our best hope is for momentary glimpses of understanding. The more we learn, the greater our unknowing. Laws of nature, like gravity or the turning earth, or electromagnetic fields, are facts; but even these we cannot fully comprehend.

From our ignorance, we will always be moving toward the light but, like those recurring dreams, never quite making the train or getting the right key to the door or being prepared for the exam. Perhaps writers are not satisfied with clichés that masquerade as truth, but must continually examine evidence and find an authentic mode of expression.

Some people tire of trying to understand. With a childlike faith, they accept without knowing. Others will always try to clean the glass and see reality more clearly. A few will throw caution to the four winds and head right into the fire and experience what it does to them. Occasionally those artists will grasp a little light and share it.

Tentative Trails

Honor the Lord with your wealth, with the firstfruits of all your crops; then your barns will be filled ...

Proverbs 3:9,10a

Computers have made writers out of many of us. Just how many remains an interesting speculation. Words scratched on a yellow pad in sloppy handwriting can be transformed into blocked, regular print on paper with some rapid keystrokes and the press of the print button. No more confusion or reading between the lines—the imprint stands very official-looking. Then the writer can make marks on the draft copy, including major reorganization trials, and accomplish a rewrite in minutes. No more rolling a new page into the typewriter, retyping, and correcting inevitable errors with the white liquid that covers mistakes. Some modern writers abandon the writing pad altogether and go straight to the screen.

The poet Donald Hall[2] is from the old school. He does not type. Every morning, he tells us, he drafts his pieces in longhand, corrects earlier poems, and takes them to the typist. Later in the day he picks up the typed copies, numbers the draft (as many as ninety trials for some pieces), and considers the poems again the next morning. Reading his poetry, I imagine the writing sessions as intense and focused. His very heart spills out from pen onto paper.

There may be a downside to easy writing on computers. More of us are writing, but most are not writing very well. I speak also of myself: I have become a sloppy typist and sometimes, I fear, a sloppy thinker. Knowing how easily words can be changed or rearranged, I don't give my whole self to the first draft. I am less careful, thoughtful, and creative than I plan to be in the end product. Where once my internal editor ruled, inhibiting all but the choicest words and phrases, the antiperfectionist has muscled in, convincing me that anything will do.

With the help of my computer I spin out volumes of mediocre stuff. Many essays never rise above their tacky beginnings. They become stuck in their tentativeness.

Anne Lamott[3] lectures and writes about "terrible first drafts," telling perfectionists there is hope even for poor starts. But those imperfect first drafts need the clear thought of a devoted writer if they are to be salvaged by revisions. The creative front end of writing is our first drive for truth-telling. Authentic. Passionate. Perceptive. Not perfectly formed but potent—with a little or a lot of fixing.

Dear God,
   Guide us to speak our truth clearly. May we offer our firstfruits to you. Amen.

Taking Time to Write

Then the Lord said to Moses, "Write this on a scroll as something to be remembered..."

Exodus 17:14a

A line from Louise DeSalvo's book, *Writing as a Way of Healing*, caught my eye: "Many people ... have told me that taking time to write seems so, well, self-indulgent, self-involved, frivolous even."[4] Since retiring "in order to write," I've had to fight my feelings, and the imagined opinions of others, that the whole writing enterprise is selfish. In the past, when personal writing time was eked out of busy workdays, it seemed more honorable. The late night or early morning efforts used time that was outside of "real" work. Now, work for pay has ended, allowing the luxury of workdays for creative writing.

Now all I have to do is quell my guilt over the things I displace because of my indulgence in writing. There are so many worthy causes that regularly tempt me to leave the desk. A sister describes me as "driven" when I am so serious about my work, and friends wonder why I don't join them for lunch. My children and young grandchildren, all within a twenty-mile radius, can use as much time as I can give.

If I were writing a novel, like a "real" writer, maybe we'd all understand. But writing short pieces such as poems and personal essays and meditations just doesn't measure up somehow. Or if I had published widely or were intent on the same, these solitary writing sessions would at least have an understandable goal.

Famous writers have often warned beginners not to write unless they have to—it is all consuming. I'll try to remember William Safire's words: "There are those who will call you a recluse—but it is better to listen to your own different drummer than to go through life with a ringing in your ears."[5]

Some days I wish I didn't have to write. But a calling doesn't often come with a justification; it is more like the commercial, "Just Do It!"

Or as the Lord's declaration to Moses, "Write this … as something to be remembered."

Dear God,
    I don't know why you called me to write. Give me strength to hush the voices in my head that would undermine your particular claim on my life. Amen.

Two-Sided Brain

My words come from an upright heart; my lips sincerely speak what I know.

Job 33:3

My father was an accomplished technical writer without ever being given that title. For eight years after giving up his medical practice, he worked for the Joint Commission on Accreditation of Healthcare Organizations (JCAHO). The commission sent out teams across the United States to check how well hospitals met the standards of care. After a two- or three-day survey, the team wrote their report. The actual writing often fell to my father. In addition, he wrote pre-survey manuals to help the hospital staff prepare for the often nerve-wracking inspections.

After Dad's death in the early 1980s, a former survey partner wrote, "His superb style of writing and lucid explanations produced the best accreditation manuals ever published ... . His spare use of words ... was a magnificent characteristic. It is easy to present a complex matter in a complex way, but infinitely more valuable to present it in an understandable way."

When I became a technical writer, my mantra was "to present complex matters in an understandable way." Although Dad had been less of a teacher to me than an example, somehow his love of language as a tool seemed also to course through my veins. Like him, I also saw the creative side of technical writing, using well chosen words to illuminate an idea. Even in a formal grant application, the applicant must demonstrate his or her passion for the beneficiaries. The right words can convey heartfelt emotion without becoming sentimental.

Although Dad wrote poetry in college, he didn't continue his creative writing after graduation. His weekly letters to all of us were as formal in tone as if he were writing an accreditation report. Only rarely did he let us see the real person behind them!

When I tried to combine a writing profession with a love of creative writing, I was conscious of the contrast of skills the two thrive on.

Technical writing is cerebral, left-brained. Its clarity relies on organization and making points with precision and persuasion. When I tried to switch gears into the creative, I realized I wanted to know where I was going before I started. Form seemed very important.

Letting go was not easy. Right-brained playfulness seemed wicked—the censor just couldn't stop judging. Giving imagination and intuition their way is easier now that I've retired from my day job. And there is always the revision stage, when I let that other brain have a crack at the piece. By then the fun-loving words are in black and white, showing that they too can bring understanding to complexity.

Loving God,

Some of us fear our own imagination. Give us eyes to see your clarifying truth everywhere. Amen

Write Now

[Jesus said] "Come with me by yourselves to a quiet place and get some rest."
Mark 6:31

It's the Memorial Day weekend and the family is away. I welcomed its coming and gladly saw my husband off on a fishing trip so that my writing time would be unfettered. From my desk I watch the gray sky and periodic downpours, feeling a little smug that I am not chasing holiday pleasures. "No parade to rain on," I think as I try to concentrate.

I put in a fidgety day and a half before taking a break to drive my mother to the cemetery to put flowers on Dad's grave. She spends the night with me; on Sunday we go to church, eat dinner together afterwards at her retirement home, and finally I head back home to revive my writing retreat. But as I drive up to the house, I see the garage door open and my husband's truck inside.

His aborted fishing trip curtails my weekend plans as well. I groan inside. Isn't this just the story of my life? Making plans and then being forced to give them up because someone needs me? Now there are meals to prepare, a pile of dirt-caked jeans to wash, and a disappointed husband to soothe. How can I ever be a serious writer in this unpredictable kind of life?

Several years ago I tried a retreat in our isolated mountain cabin in Colorado. My husband, the dog, and I arrived a few days before he left for a conference. Not one to be fearful alone, I was almost giddy with the possibilities of producing some significant writing in four days of solitude. I sat at my desk facing the mountains and waited to be transported.

But the log house creaked and moaned; the dog was no company; the few groceries I brought didn't interest me. Spring's short days with no car, no TV, and terrible radio reception left me unable to find any break from solitude. Instead of being inspired from within, I was depleted from without. Excitement turned to guilt at wasting a rare and beautiful opportunity to write my heart out.

It is Memorial Day. The one I thought I'd be spending in quiet. The washer is whirring, the dog is begging to play, my husband is in a stew because it's still raining and he's discovered that the phone is dead. We are isolated, but there is no peace.

Today I own this as my life: always in the middle of things, pulled one way and then another. But my pen is rolling. Who needs a retreat? I think I'll go make some potato salad and invite my husband to an indoor holiday picnic.

Dear God,

Inspire my response to real life—the messy, noisy, complex one you know is right for me. Amen.

Old

Hearing the free-flowing nostalgia read aloud by members of our New-Age Writing Group—spiced with comments about "kids nowadays" who will never know the wonder of simpler times of one-gift Christmases, house calls by the country doctor, and joy rides in the rumble seat of a Model-T Ford—I want to shout: "Our children are building their own memories," which I imagine will one day be as simply grand as ours, as they decry the younger generation of privilege in their own sanitized, glorified, gospelized, petrified, adulterated true stories, duly read aloud to the white heads of the Newest-Age Writing Group.

Tips, Hints, and Advice

Do not "overwrite" by using more words than needed— circle all words that pad or puff up your writing and delete them.

1. My daughter thought of the name for my business—First Draft Consulting. As time went by I understood the wisdom of calling it "first" rather than "last" draft. Naturally the first draft was not the one I showed my clients, but it recorded forever the front end of creativity. The essence was always there, even if more work was needed.

2. I seldom leave a book unfinished, both because I choose carefully and because I love a story, any story. However, one sure spoiler is "overwriting," or writing with more words than are necessary. Flowery, overly descriptive, obscure words don't keep me with the page, they chase me away. I feel like I'm in a freshman creative writing class, where writers are writing to impress, not express. For my taste, plain and to the point is best. Take a piece of your writing. Circle all words that pad or puff up your message. Delete.

3. Nostalgia may be fun for you and may be an instant connection to your age-mates, but it makes for boring reading unless there are some redeeming qualities. Don't label the old days good or bad; just make them come to life in the act of storytelling. That two-mile walk to and from school in all kinds of weather (without shoes) will need to include what you heard, saw, smelled, and tasted along the way to adventure.

4. One reason that I began writing meditations is that they are a legitimate form for expressing faith. In other nonfiction the challenge is to write as a Christian, but bring it off with authenticity. Writers of fiction can always put words into their characters' mouths to deliver messages that

would otherwise appear dogmatic if they came from the author. In this book I include essays with no overt spiritual theme and meditations that contain experiential faith. Some subjects lend themselves to spiritual reflection; others do not. Let the reader or listener be led to your truth, not ambushed by it. C. S. Lewis called it *Surprised by Joy.*[6]

5. In proposal-writing workshops I have taught, the first task revolves around practice in basic writing, the kind most of us learned in grade school. For technical writing we consider tense, paragraphs, and lead sentences; and I always promote active voice. While especially important to those for whom English is a second or third language (as it was with a group of Kenyans I taught recently), every writer needs to use words wisely. Strong verbs and descriptive nouns with their modifiers add depth to your work without adding unnecessary length. Look over a piece of your writing. Can any noun be more specific? Can any verb be replaced with one that shows the action more clearly? Choose your words with care. In any kind of writing, your word choices make the piece lose luster—or they make it shine.

Writing Challenge

3

Write an essay, poem, or short story using one hundred or fewer of your choicest words.

The one-hundred-word essay entitled "Old" that appeared earlier in this chapter was written for a publication that specified that unbearable word limit. Each issue of *One Hundred Words* prescribed only one word as the basis for pieces of writing to be considered. I used these exercises especially for writing practice.

Many people have told me that it is much easier to write long than short. The word limit exercise helps us to weigh each word and make sure it pulls its weight. It must contribute to the meaning of the piece or be left behind. No filler, no fluff, just words that contain meaning.

Despite the word limit, you will notice a clear point of view in the essay, "Old." I take a jab at the "truth" of true stories. I try writing a whole essay in one long sentence. (Grammar check always objects!) To save words, the essay utilizes a list of words that hint at meaning rather than explain it.

When you write for publication, you will frequently face the oppression of "word counts." For practice, *write an essay, poem or (very) short story* using only one hundred of your choicest words. I offer the word *idol*, which I have just chosen at random from the dictionary. Make of this word what you will—but don't let your piece contain even one more than one hundred words.

Realism

If the personal essay frequently presents a middle-aged point of view, it may be because it is the fruit of ripened experience, which naturally brings with it some worldly disenchantment or at least realism. With middle age also comes a taste for equilibrium, that stubborn, almost unnerving calm that so often pervades the personal essay.

Montaigne exemplified the melancholy, stoical balance of middle age: "I have seen the grass, the flower, and the fruit; now I see the dryness—happily since it is naturally—which is, for better or worse, the by-product of a developed sense of selfhood."

Phillip Lopate[1]

4

A writer must work out of what is—not from ideal circumstances. The happily-ever-after that completes every fairly tale is rarely part of his story. Troubles have come and troubles have gone, and the adult no longer imagines that all days will be rosy and hardship will never come his way. By midlife, some dreams of accomplishment or fame have already been set aside, especially if they required a fit body. But, despite failure to meet an ideal of one's own making, the writer calmly testifies to uncommon blessings. The road not taken does not conjure regret but understanding. The road traveled, with all its minute detail, is far more interesting than the might-have-beens.

The personal essay offers the writer a forum for honesty—about self, other people, and places of the heart. In contrast to this middle-aged point of view, of which Lopate speaks, is that of some older persons. Things were always better back in the old days. Good always triumphed over evil. Cantankerous grandpas or husbands, now long gone, mellowed into nice guys. Today's children and prices and relationships are really out of line.

The writer of personal essays (see Chapter 8) must write true things as she has experienced them. Many of us are tempted to let the past simply pass. But it is in facing the reality of the hidden parts of our lives that we achieve the equanimity of maturity. We've chased rainbows—caught a few and thought we could forget the ones we missed. But sometimes the human drama is found in those confusing, frustrating, and unnerving events that we live to tell about.

If a story is to have the ring of truth, it must be multifaceted, not one-dimensional. We've all heard stories that are just "too good to be true." No one I know lives in a perfect home or has the perfect family. The euphoria of such an existence would leave little room for speculation or examination—nothing to write home about. By revisiting our failures as well as our foibles we come to know our selves. A good novel is colored by complex characters; a good memoir lets our complex lives connect at a basic level with the lives of others.

What follows are three meditations and an essay about what I know, on writing and life.

Interference

The actual process of writing ... demands complete, noiseless privacy, without even music: A baby howling two blocks away will drive me nuts.

William Styron[2]

There are ten of us staying here in the mountain cabin, ranging in age from five to seventy-three. People come and go constantly but gather *en masse* for meals, when the weather turns rainy, or as night falls. Fishing for trout is good this year, so at any one time half of the cabin's inhabitants could be at the stream. I do my share of going, but my desk in the loft calls me even during the confusion. Each day, by some heavenly wonder, I find myself alone in the cabin for an hour or two.

The CD plays a lovely Bach collection designed especially as background music. After five minutes, I realize I am distracted even by good music. Off it goes. For writing, my mind has only one track, and that appears only in quiet. Out comes the pen and on goes my muse—just like that. I didn't count on a noise-free place this week, but I welcome it right now. No dogs, no babies, no TV—just short spurts of solitude.

Many of us pre-television learners can do only one thing at a time. My children can usually do three—read, watch, and talk—at once. Noise is particularly bothersome to me; TV commercials drive me crazy.

Quiet is not just my preference; it is my necessity. For some time I've known I cannot weed out extraneous sound. A doctor says it's a neurological condition that doesn't allow me to focus on important sounds—they all come in at the same intensity. In one work setting, my assigned office had walls that didn't reach to ceiling. After a few weeks of accomplishing nothing but eavesdropping on conversations all around me, I begged for another room. I adapted easily to a storage room not much bigger than a closet.

Mom complains about her hearing aids, "They just make everything louder." I know the frustration. Those darn buzzing fans, clicking clocks, tapping fingers, barking dogs, snoring neighbors, and dripping rain are just not welcome in my writing space.

Speaking of rain—it has just begun, thumping steadily on our metal roof. Soon the fisherpeople will stream in for cover, the hikers will shorten their trip, and the outdoor games will be replaced by board games. But never mind, I've had my island of quiet. Let the rumpus begin.

Spirit of God,
You have taught me to work around my limitations. Thank you for making your appearance when the time is ripe. Amen.

Writing and Running

But those who hope in the Lord … they will run and not grow weary, they will walk and not be faint.

Isaiah 40:31

The East Lansing (Michigan) 10K Race was the most talked about one on the runners' circuit. Highly organized and publicized, the competition drew some big names. Roads were cordoned off to hold back the spectators. Two weeks before, I ran my first 10K and placed—not too difficult in the Over-40 women's bracket—but I was full of myself. I signed up.

The passion to run began as I watched my daughter run track in high school. I was overwhelmed by desire, even though I lacked everything a runner needs. Slowly, over many months of solo pushing, I was able to run the six-mile loop in my neighborhood. What began with no thoughts of competition changed with that little piece of metal they gave me.

Waiting at the starting line for the East Lansing Race, I noticed a woman who had placed first in my division the week before. The gun sounded, and we fell in running together. Her pace was slightly faster, so I unconsciously tried for several miles to keep up. At the top of a rise that left me puffing, I motioned for her to go ahead. On the downhill, I still tried to keep her pace. Rounding a corner in a kind of a daze, I heard someone shouting and vaguely recognized my children's voices. The noise seemed muffled as if in a giant amphitheater, as I ran erratically and finally stumbled toward the grassy parkway. My knees buckled; I collapsed.

A rescue unit appeared, rushed me by ambulance to the ER, tested all my vital signs, and released me to a bewildered family who had watched in vain for me to cross the finish line. My problem—simple hyperventilation. Apparently, I pushed myself to keep up, breathing fast and shallow, robbing me of needed oxygen.

The scene came back to me more than twenty years later when I read a quote by the screenwriter, Paul Schrader, "Feel the pages under you the same way a runner feels the gravel under his feet."[3]

I had always suspected there was a connection between writing and running. Ah, the memory of running: the wind, the gravelly road, the sky, offering me incredible freedom. Ah, the joy of writing: a pen that rolls to the right down a line, the air charged with electric thought, and the smooth white paper offering no resistance as my hand slides over its surface—onward.

If only I can remember to breathe deeply and work at my own pace.

Dear God,

I praise you for putting desire in my heart to try what seems impossible. When I am weary and faint—inspire me again. Amen.

Hawking Your Wares

I don't know what it would be like not to be a writer. Part of the reason I became a writer was because in dealing with ordinary problems, my imagination is usually quite deficient.

Anne Beattie[4]

Sandy, our mailwoman on the rural route, always delivers the box of accumulated mail after a vacation hold. She comes down our long driveway, deposits the heavy box by the door, and rings the bell. We chat for a while; I can't thank her enough for her kindness.

The box is heavy—weighted down by catalogues and magazines. When they arrive two a day, the effect is not as great. But when I sift through newsmagazines, literary journals, the writers' helps, and the church periodical, I feel under siege—not by the information, but by the mountain of tagboard enclosures that fill each magazine and ruin my day.

Leafing through to find the good reads is stymied by all those pesky inserts hanging onto the center spine. Like a succession of hurdles on a track, I must leap each one before I can read what I paid for. The stack of worthless garbage piles at my feet as I fume. Don't the publishers know how irritating it is to be urged repeatedly to subscribe when I already have? Just as seeing the same TV commercial three times in rapid succession or hearing a too loud voice repeating a toll-free number makes me want to boycott the product rather than buy it, I am ready to unsubscribe. Couldn't magazines have one run for subscribers and another for the newsstands?

Perhaps my religious periodical won't give in to such foolishness. But no, even it contains a paid insert by a mission agency on stiffer paper and a gift envelope attached. And the newspaper, especially on Sunday with advertising fliers tucked in everywhere, enough already. Even *TV Guide* is hardly recognizable under flaps and fillers. A few weeks ago a new twist: extra-long pages full of ads hang out the right side, making it impossible to leaf through and locate any show's date or time.

Incredibly, even the dog-eared copies of last year's magazines in doctors' offices still contain those obnoxious inserts. Am I the only one annoyed, disgusted, and grousing? Am I alone in loving the feel of paperbacks and magazines, the way I can let the pages ruffle under my thumb on the first perusal?

Hawking wares never really works—at least for people like me. Give us a miniscule ad on page forty-seven tucked between two good book reviews and we'll jump up, make a call, and buy something we don't need.

Dear God,
 Help me accept the things I cannot change. Amen.

Squatter's Rights

The task of a writer is to soak up dibs and dabs of this and that, swish them around in the mind, and slowly release words or marks in a thin stream across a page. The gathering happens anywhere; the letting go needs a certain kind of place. Some writers prefer to work in cafés where life swirls nearby; others near a window overlooking crowded streets or countryside beauty. While I have made the best of airports, cafeterias, picnic benches, study halls, and kitchen tables, I yearn for a place of absolute quiet, free from anything that catches my eye or ear and halts the flow of words from my mind to the waiting paper. At least in the beginning. I have great difficulty ignoring sounds until the volume of my inner voice drowns out exterior noise. Some days, when in my solitary space the outpouring begins, not in trickles but in torrents, even an explosion in the next room would not interrupt. My writer's voice demands to be my only suitor.

I discovered a perfect place for writing at about the same time I gave in to the urge to write. To get there I must hike along a ridge next to a steep bank leading down to a stream. I search for a safe place to descend so as not to slip on loose gravel or rely on a shaky rock step. The Carbonate Creek calls me—most days as bubbling water sliding smoothly over and around the rocks, noisy without being intrusive. But the high banks, now a short distance from the water's edge, tell the history of high water in spring and even mud floods in which waves of debris, silt, and murky water tear down everything in its path. But I have come in summer, when the dry Colorado air snatches the creek's spray in flight. I pick my way to water's edge and then follow it upstream to my desk—a large flat rock tilted away from the sun. Beside me runs water music that feeds my spirit; around are mountains and overhead blue sky with only a wisp of cloud.

No one knows where I have gone, for the mountain cabin from which I've come is full of people who think they need me. I feel like

Madeleine L'Engle[5] sneaking off from Crosswicks to her "circle of quiet." I pray for the same kinds of results. Several hours later, as the sun lowers, I pick my way up the bank refreshed. Back at the house, my random gathering of pieces resumes.

In winter, when I am far away, the creek bank is covered with snow, leaving no hint of my sun-warmed desk. I'm forced indoors too. I choose a library. What it lacks in ambiance, it makes up in atmosphere—books, magazines, newspapers—even the information highway—surround me like a "cloud of witnesses." I listen to their voices without reading their words so that I can turn to my own book, the one in my head. Today I find a study carrel in a college library, with its three bland walls surrounding the writing surface. The walls do their job, keeping me focused on important things. But when two students with other priorities greet each other nearby, compare notes, and playfully try to impress each other, I gather my papers and move out of earshot. I settle in a new cubicle, closer to the sunlight and warmed by a nearby heater vent. Words surface again.

I've known libraries everywhere I've been and never met one I didn't like. As a child, I was sometimes allowed to stop at the public library on my walk home from school, a detour of about three blocks. I could not read well, but I soaked up the wisdom of the ages in a little alcove decorated with a picture of a large bird flying, the wings outstretched, carrying a little girl on its back. I've been riding on that mighty bird ever since, into university libraries in Michigan, Cleveland, Vancouver, Amsterdam, Iowa City, assorted community libraries, and even mobile and mall libraries.

While writing, I enjoy the company of books. The memory of old oak tables, bankers' lamps, and wooden card catalogues endures even in stark modern libraries. Sometimes when words don't flow, I browse the stacks, where often a title entices me, only to discover inside some tidbit that gets my writing unstuck. I think of it as kind of writer's roulette—some cylinder eventually fires. But libraries close; and, today at least, one man and one dog hope I come home before supper.

But now, at last, there is a place that never closes and the light never fades; a place I call my own, my idea of perfection on earth. I've spent a lifetime searching for this "room of my own," as Virginia Woolf prescribed for every writer. From shared bedrooms as a child, to college dorms, to the corner of a bedroom or space in my husband's study—I have graduated. Since retirement, I work in a small blue room on the second floor of the house we built a year ago. My husband picked a space on the lower lever with a clear view of the woods, wildlife, and the now frozen lake. But too much beauty or duty distracts me. Friends question my decision to hunker down with my back to the high windows of my room. The radio is silent and my computer hums only after the thinking is nailed down by pen on paper. I treasure the gift of quiet, knowing full well it comes with age and privilege but also exacts its own dues. "To whom much is given, much will be required … ."

My desk is cluttered—stacks of paper, dozens of books, tools, tissues, sticky-notes, a nail clipper, *Poets and Writers* opened to an author interview, a full Diet Coke and empties alongside, a datebook, the computer monitor, my Bible, a half-full backpack—just stuff, good stuff, my stuff. All I need is a clearing big enough for my sketchbook. This chaos is my own. A few feet away under a pastoral Van Gogh print stands a bookcase for my current favorites. By design, my other precious books gathered over time are in a hall library where they can't tempt me, begging to be opened once more. Behind the desk chair, under the windows that backlight the room, crowds a long line of writing notebooks, silent witnesses to the fact that I am a writer.

On days when my little room or the library carrel or the creekside space is crowded with critics and naysayers whispering, "You can't!" "You wouldn't!" "That's dumb!" I call on the words of writing mentor, Anne Lamott.[6] Together we smile and, politely but forcefully, tell them all to leave.

I have squatter's rights. This is my place.

Tips, Hints, and Advice

Think about the details of your ideal writing life. Write them down. Check once a month and see how the picture changes.

1. In my experience, writing is like running—two of the hardest things I've ever done. Just to keep going draws on all the fortitude, endurance, and cleverness within. Deficiencies of time and talent tempt me to try something easier. "Why put yourself through this?" says that voice within. "You've worked hard all your life—relax for a change." What is writing *like* for you? Go ahead and write out that likeness.

2. The University of Iowa, well known for its Master of Fine Arts program in creative writing, has offered a Summer Festival of Writing for the past fifteen years. Aspiring writers elect a class (one week or one weekend) from a roster of ten or twelve per session. The twelve class members are a cross-section of age, experience, and region of origin and residence. In memoir classes, old and young capitalize on memories, be it of nineteen years or ninety years. If Montaigne[7] is right about personal essays, we might ask how long it takes to produce fruit from "ripened experience." When I was young, I loved but rarely reflected on that life. Being in class with very talented and perceptive college students has opened my eyes. Age has nothing to do with reflection. Anyone can look back and write about the real world, as experienced.

3. Taking off their tinted glasses may be hard for Christians, always in a hurry to get to the good news. But if your reader cannot experience the struggle or deep sorrow with you, how will she be able to feel the joy? And if the ending is unhappy, reflect long and hard before you rejoice. Or just record your assurance that despair will

not last forever and you never face difficulties alone. Happy endings warm us, but are they the stuff of real life?

4. Make a list of things that really tick you off, like the tag board insets do to me. Your negative emotions might surprise you. Which of them will you write about today?

5. Finding a *"place just right"* as the old Shaker hymn suggests, is more than that physical space in which your writing blossoms. Place is also a comfort in finding your spiritual home—a state of being that brings *shalom*, peace. Place, for all its sense of well-being, is not a hiding place where one goes to hibernate. Describe your physical and spiritual place.

6. New writers often think there is some magic formula for writing success, that revolves around method or process. "How many pages per day?" "How long is your average writing session?" "What time of day is best?" Or a magical tool, like sharp pencils or rolling ballpoint pens, or a keyboard facing a dark screen. I have gotten beyond the "trick" stage of the trade, but am still fascinated by the writing life. A seminal book for me was John Jerome's, *The Writing Trade: A Year in the Life*.[8] He drew a picture of his life, full of down-to-earth, very unromantic detail. Each of us will amass our own particular detail. Think ahead about the details of your ideal writing life. Write them down. Make a reality check once a month and see how the picture changes.

Writing Challenge

4

Take us into your writing place. Give the reader a tour of your mind or your pen at work, and the conditions necessary to make both work.

The quote used at the beginning of this chapter hints that "reality" or "worldly disenchantment" is the fruit of ripened experience. Believers of every age know, sooner or later, that this world is not "home." We lost the perfect garden soon after inhabiting it and have been unable to reinvent or reclaim it. However, the vocation of writing can restore a sense of place in this world.

In the essay "Squatter's Rights," I talk about a perfect place to write. The fact that it is beside a swift stream and the desk is a rock does not ruin my idea of perfection. My little place served me well at a time in my life when writing was only a romantic dream. Now, this place is more of a monument than a workspace. It represents all the longing and resolve and wildness that my mind can harness for writing.

Today, take us to the place or places you write. Combining the themes of place and real life, create pictures for us with words. *Take us into your place.* Give the reader a tour of your mind or your pen at work, and the conditions necessary to make both work. Be *real* as you show us what happens in your place. Could it be a foretaste of a lasting home?

Meaning

And as I listen to the silence, I learn that my feelings about art and feelings about the Creator of the Universe are inseparable. To try to talk about art and about Christianity is for me one and the same thing, and it means attempting to share the meaning of my life, what gives it, for me, its tragedy and its glory. It is what makes me respond to the death of an apple tree, the birth of a puppy, northern lights shaking the sky, by writing stories.

Madeleine L'Engle[1]

5

You might call it the indirect approach: sharing the meaning of your life through reflection on a dying tree, an animal's birth or a natural wonder. A direct approach to conveying meaning would be one of definitions, facts, and proof-texts: Life is _____; death is _____; beauty is _____.

The explanatory approach may seem more clear at first. But then along comes the death of *your* spouse, the rescue of the last three pups in *your* Irish setter's litter, or that golden ball of a harvest moon. Then only the indirect path will lead you anywhere near meaning.

Writers have always searched for words to describe feeling. But words often fail and the best we can do is to approach meaning by showing what the emotion laden experience is like. Is there something we know well that can help us glimpse a mystery of something we do not yet know? Or, failing that, perhaps the only thing that can be told is what this experience is *not* like.

Victor Frankel, a holocaust survivor, spent a lifetime trying to show the indescribable. *Man's Search for Meaning*[2] is his classic example of a journey that is every man's journey. God's Spirit infuses our life with meaning; the Spirit stands ready to do the same with our words, at times with meaning greater than we can know. In turn, our words can be used by God to show his presence and power in the lives of our readers.

See and Tell

Only be careful, and watch yourselves closely so that you do not forget the things your eyes have seen or let them slip from your heart ...

Deuteronomy 4:9a

Telling Your Stories—On Paper" was the title I chose for the class. On the first day twelve men and women, age sixty to eighty, gathered in a circle of college desks. The slight discomfort they projected as they faced each other soon gave way to openness.

"This is not a class about writing," I boldly declared. "This is a course *for* writing. I expect a fresh piece of writing at each class, one of which you will rewrite after we learn something about memoirs."

My first task, I supposed while preparing the syllabus, would be to convince each person that he or she had the ability to write. But not one balked at the first free-write; I watched as their pens rolled confidently across the page. I had underestimated the boldness of these eager storytellers.

Perhaps their hardest task came in choosing which stories to write from among a lifetime of experiences. The assignments I gave helped them walk through ideas, but then they ran. By the third week, I could see from my place in the circle that each person had fresh writing displayed on the desk. Although I heard the usual disclaimers before each reading; ("This isn't very good,") not a person refused to read, read tentatively, or had to run to the bathroom before reading.

I imposed a nonthreatening method of critique. I asked the class to evaluate each piece they heard with the following questions: What words or phrases stuck? (I call these Velcro words) How does the writing make you feel? What more do you need to know? Quick responses and lively comments characterized their feedback to each other. I promised them my own critique but, after the first week, I found they wanted more than mechanics. They wanted judgment: Is this writing good or bad? Am I a good storyteller? But I declined to judge their heartfelt writing. With these mature writers, my job was to coach and cheer, not to grade.

I could almost see the wheels turning inside their graying heads as they listened to each other read. They were looking beyond each tale—comparing it with their own, seeing their own correctable flaws, and understanding for themselves what makes a good story. In time, they became their own best judges. They laughed and cried at their own words. They continued to fill long, quiet days by telling wonderful stories—on paper.

Dear God,

Thank you for giving us stories that help us to discover meaning in our lives. Give us boldness to tell them to people we care about. Amen.

The Finger Writes

Suddenly the fingers of a human hand appeared and wrote on the plaster of the wall, near the lampstand in the royal palace. The king watched the hand as it wrote.

Daniel 5:5

I just reread the book of Daniel in one sitting to remember the context of the famous handwriting-on-the-wall story. Along with my classmates, the stories of Daniel thrilled me from my earliest days in Sunday school. He was our first superhero. He owned magical powers: knowing the king's dreams and their meaning, refusing to follow orders but still winning, sleeping unharmed beside ravenous lions, and understanding words on a wall in an unknown language. The first chapters of Daniel read like a novel.

Besides the plunder from conquered Jerusalem, Nebuchadnezzar, the king of Babylon, drafted the ablest and brightest young men. Like today's scholar athletes, they had to be smart and physically able. With all that potential, the king planned to teach them Babylon's "language and literature" (v.1:4b). He even wanted to dictate the high protein diet available at the training table. Daniel and friends thrived even though they preferred vegetables. Daniel distinguished himself by deciphering the meaning of dreams.

When Belshazzar became king in place of his debilitated father, he decided to use the gold and silver goblets from the temple at a banquet. As the cups of wine were passed among thousands of nobles and their harems, the people raised a toast to their manmade gods. In the dim and flickering light of an elevated lamp, the one true God chose to use a plain plaster wall. Nothing like a lightshow at a rock concert, but enough to get the attention of the enormous audience. When the king saw the hand making unreadable words, his knees buckled and he keeled over in front of all the guests.

After the wise men of the land failed to decipher the code, the queen remembered Daniel's extraordinary powers. She convinced the king to summon Daniel and beg for the words' meanings in exchange for gifts. "Keep the stuff but I'll tell you the meaning," Daniel might have said, right ready with the sermon. "The hand didn't appear out of the blue—there is God-history here. You ignored your own father's madness and God's sovereignty. Your forgetting will cost your life and the kingdom."[3]

The words of the hand came true that very night. Belshazzar was slain.

Like many good stories, the context of "The handwriting on the wall" has been lost, and the phrase itself has become a cliché. Getting direction, knowing the future, gaining otherworldly intervention have all become part of its meaning, but writers do well to remember God's story before alluding to "the hand." God's meaning and message await our discovery through the biblical mosaic of words, stories, parables, and songs.

Dear God,

Show us the way by your hand, voice, word, command, and history. Give us the grace to follow. Amen.

God Wrote

When Moses went up on the mountain, the cloud covered it, and the glory of the Lord settled on Mount Sinai. For six days the cloud covered the mountain, and on the seventh day the Lord called to Moses from within the cloud.

Exodus 24:15,16

God told Moses to meet him so he could give the Israelites' leader the stone tablets on which were written, in God's own hand, the law, the commandments, and instructions for living. Moses trekked up the mountain, reached the cloud, and waited to be invited in. God made him wait. God made him wait a long time; at least, to me, six days seems a long time to "do nothing." That's an entire work week plus a Saturday. I know Moses left his judicial work with Aaron and Hur, but accustomed as he was to a busy court docket that filled both days and evenings, the wait must have seemed interminable. God had not told Moses in advance how long he would wait, so I doubt that he brought anything to help him pass the time. The cloud was there, so God could not be far away; all he could do was wait.

Finally, God called. "Come on into my cloud," he might have said. "Come into my presence," is what he meant. Because of their special relationship, God and Moses shared a space, and neither was diminished. For more than a month they worked together. It must have been like a writing retreat—no distractions, no other agenda—just a concerted effort to make a permanent record.

But for the people of Israel, the wait was too long. As weeks became a month, they gave up on seeing Moses again. The Lord may have decided to keep him forever. Aaron either gave up hope or yielded to the harangue of the people: "Okay, okay—you may have a shiny object to rally around, since God has been quiet and you no longer trust the cloud."

You know the rest of the story: the forty days of writing smashed into unreadable fragments. The record of God's plan was in shambles; he vowed to leave the people in disarray.

But Moses knew the value of the written word. He put his reputation with God on the line for the sake of that permanent word. Words matter. They last. They give us hope.

Dear God,

Thank you for listening to Moses's bold begging. Millennia later we still have your commands. Amen.

Slain by the Spirit

The Spirit of God has made me; the breath of the Almighty gives me life.

Job 33:4

It is Pentecost Sunday; red banners hang above the podium. The purple of Easter has been replaced by the red of the Holy Spirit's fire. Ordination of church office bearers happens today, and I am among them. I see the deep red, and I long to be filled anew with the Spirit. The congregation sings the chorus, *"Come, o come and fill this temple ... with the glory of the Lord."*[4] I hold my hand open, palm upward, and believe God will fill me with whatever I need.

We are asked to reaffirm our faith and accept the office, saying, "I do, God helping me." We kneel on the podium step while those leaving office, "lay on hands." I feel two strong hands on my shoulder, and I can sense the Spirit's power rushing into my waiting body. I long to stay in the moment.

But the others are rising long before I am ready. I stand up, suddenly aware of the congregation watching but not feeling the Spirit as I am right now. I rush to leave the front and rejoin my family. But as I go, the others remain; I alone have forgotten the directions to stay for the charge to the officers. I do not hear my commission, as the red of Pentecost rises on the back of my neck.

For years I was part of a multicultural fellowship, where we were urged regularly to pray for the Spirit's presence during a lively worship. Shouts of praise came whenever members could let themselves be stirred by God to the point of raising hands or even, occasionally, dancing in the aisles. Some Christian fellowships pray to be "slain" by the Spirit. In my new congregation I sense the need for a less boisterous spirit, one that enters the head while the rest of the body stays in control.

Now it is Pentecost Monday. Alone in my study, I ask the Spirit to come again and bless my writing. It is safer for the Spirit to descend when I am alone, not trying to follow directions. The music from yesterday echoes, *"Come Holy Spirit, Heavenly Dove, with all your quickening power ... ."*[5] I close my eyes and wait for the Spirit to quicken me like an infant in the womb. I'm open to the Spirit—a little singing or dancing, "hallelujahs," or very free, free-writes—in the solitude of my room.

Spirit of God,
    Come into my heart. Give me words. Breathe your spirit upon me. Amen.

Tips, Hints, and Advice

Learn to critique your own work. Put a piece of your writing away for several weeks and then reread it with new eyes. Is it ready for a showing, a touchup, or a total rewrite? The choice is yours.

1. There has always been debate over the origin of sacred texts. Someone had to write them before someone could read them. How they were inspired, composed, and edited remains a mystery. The same mystery blankets our writing. Where did that idea originate? Who put it on my mind and heart at this time? Why do I need to transform it and show it to others? Work within the mystery of your own writing until it finds its place in God's plan.

2. To improve as a writer, you must learn to critique your own work; writing groups and classes don't happen often enough. Put a piece of your writing away for several weeks and then read it with new eyes. Ask yourself what words and phrases still stick like Velcro and sound fresh. How does your own story, poem, or memoir make you feel? Imagine someone you know reading it. Would that person need more detail to make the article satisfying and complete? Be charitable but realistic. You may opt for total rewrite, or you may judge it ready for other eyes.

3. When other writers critique your work they often see themes and subplots that you never consciously intended. Perhaps the remarks help you see the meaning of the story or essay. You can decide if the new theme needs to become more prominent or less. The critique may lead to a whole new piece of writing.

Writing Challenge

5

Writing about a time when you faced a life crisis, show us how you searched for new meaning. Read your work to another person and let that person's comments be the basis for revisions.

Although writing is a solitary pursuit, no one can really do it alone. Even a recluse like Emily Dickinson had contacts with people and nature, if only by looking out her window or writing letters. Most of us need to be among people and activity in order to collect the material we will transform into something new. Thoreau certainly had to know the world of Concord before he could protest its complexity and form an alternative.

Famous writers and thinkers through the years have been part of lively discussion groups. C.S. Lewis and J.R.R. Tolkien had the Inklings, Virginia Woolf the Bloomsbury Group, and Robert Penn Warren the Fugitive Group. Most writers do need other eyes to periodically review their work and give comment. The first step may be as part of a writing class, where your writing can be heard and considered by other writers. Some writers' groups allow would-be writers to join. But as you get a sense of your interests, type of writing, and relative level of accomplishment, you may want to find just one partner or two whom you trust to give you a reality check and to keep you writing. If you are expected to bring one or more stories or a certain number of pages to your group, there will be less temptation to let other interests crowd out your writing time.

Write about a time when you faced a life crisis or challenge in which beliefs and your approach to problems did not provide the meaning or clarity you needed to get through this event. Show how you searched for and found new meaning. Read your work to at least one other person and let that person's comments be the basis for revisions.

Hopefulness

Things are going well—words are flowing and then glowing, getting better with each hour or day, and in your mind the manuscript is nothing short of marvelous, unquestionably the best stuff you've ever done ... Then one morning you pick up this priceless piece of copy and read it again, expecting it to knock off your socks.

Instead you find yourself wanting to throw up, or throw it out. The examples you loved, quivered over as you smoothed them into the manuscript, now are stone cold dead. The manuscript seems stiff and wordy; there are things that don't seem to fit and some of it doesn't even make sense.

Don Aslett and Carol Cartaino[1]
Get Organized, Get Published

6

"H ope against hope" is a phrase that often describes my attitude toward my first drafts. The pages are best left untouched for a while after coming out of my eager mind. First writing must stew in its juices for a while. Sometimes "leftovers" taste better the next day or week if frozen, but at other times the opposite is true. You can have two similarly distinct reactions to your writing after time has passed, too: better than you remembered, or tasteless junk.

Our job is to know the difference. I've had it both ways. When it is good, I sometimes doubt I really wrote it. When it is bad, I'm sure elves composed it while I slept.

The good part is that drafts are changeable, not while they rest but when you consider ways to make them better. The bad part is you may too quickly burn them. Any first work contains lots of passion, even if the prose is flawed. The careful editor, yourself or another, can clarify and tweak but cannot recreate the initial ideas that formed the piece. A seasoned writer will neither regard the raw stuff as total junk or a sparkling jewel, but some gradation in between. Don't let the judge rob your work of a fair trail. Changes can be made; changes *must* be made.

Publish or Perish

But the man who had received one talent went off, dug a hole in the ground and hid his master's money.

Matthew 25:18

Author Anne Lamott says that publishing is overrated. Those of us on the short side of writing success smile and think, "*She* can say that." But Lamott insists that the real joy of writing comes not when it finally appears in print, but while it is being created. Readers are important because they buy books, but the truth of our words does not change when they are published. Good work comes from an expressive heart, not as the fulfillment of a formula or in response to the public's changing taste.[2]

Many of us who are writing as a second or umpteenth career hate to think about publishing. We simply don't know where to begin. I, for one, began writing with no thought of publication. "This is just for me and perhaps a few friends," I reasoned. But the volume increased, especially when I made writing more than a hobby. With more time and attention to craft, the pressure to go public intensified.

In April 2000, several writer friends were my houseguests during a three-day conference, the Festival of Faith and Writing at Calvin College in Grand Rapids.[3] We talked publication. None of us could understand what distinguished a published author from an unpublished writer—each of us recalling the best work of the other. My husband listened. After they left, he wanted to talk. Hearing my friends' comments about my writing, he began to take it more seriously. For him to urge me toward publication was quite a step. For me, more pressure.

So I study the markets in *Poets and Writers* and *Christian Writer's Market Guide*[4] and the Internet. I leave time after exhilarating writing sessions to do the grunt work, making decisions about what and where and then jump through the hoops each one has erected in order to get an audience.

Even though my "tenure" doesn't depend on publication as it does in academia, I have to agree with Madeline L'Engle:

> *The writer does want to be published; the painter urgently hopes that someone will see the finished canvas ... the composer needs his music to be heard. Art is communication, and if there is no communication it is as though the work had been stillborn.*[5]

Wanting to be heard is as natural as wanting to make noise. The tree falling alone in a forest may never even make a sound.

Dear God,
  Reassure me that gifts are meant to be shared, not buried. Show me the way. Amen.

Hope against Hope

Remember your word to your servant, for you have given me hope.

Psalm 119:49

H ow to get Your Nonfiction Book Published" is the title of one midday lecture at the Iowa Summer Writing Festival. I file in with the others, trying to hide my eagerness to learn just how to get this publishing thing done. The room fills with "wannabes" just like me—fledgling writers filled with passion for their subjects and their craft. We are people who would someday like to see many pages bound in either board or paper with our names on the front. A young man, whose wife is in my afternoon class, just gave up his law practice to write a novel. Even the instructor of the workshop I am taking is present; not out of courtesy I think, but because she too wants to continue to publish.

As the hour passes I get less hopeful. The speaker tells his story of finding a hot-button topic, knowing some people, schmoozing with editors and agents, and getting good advice in negotiating a contract. His training in journalism taught him to write fast, so the required revisions and total section rewrites didn't faze him. I've met enough writers here and elsewhere to know we are more often plodders than speed demons. We share an unfounded optimism that good writing will somehow be recognized and promoted, saving us from having to "toot our own horn."

After the lecture, the ex-lawyer reminds me that this was only one person's experience. His hope is still alive. His wife, who has promoted his career-changing decision with all its uncertainty, has not yet formed a more realistic perspective. Their stakes are higher than mine.

Each year after my week at the Iowa Festival, I go into a slump. I can hardly bring myself to the desk to incorporate into my writing even the helpful critiques I received from my peers. So many writers, so many words, so much competition. So I spend time in libraries and bookstores, browsing. Soon I am following a trail of interest and making my choices for borrowing and buying. A large used-book section in one store entices me to the Nonfiction "Writing" shelf. I cannot resist.

Suddenly I am reminded that behind each book I hold is an author who was, one day, also unpublished. And that person, like me, loves books and buys books and is never saturated. Something magical always happens when writer and reader meet.

I believe in magic. That keeps hope alive.

Dear God,

You know our longing to make stories and be blessed by them. Your Book is filled with stories that give our lives meaning. Ora et labora[6]. *Amen.*

A Fly on the Wall

Let death take my enemies by surprise; let them go down alive to the grave, for evil finds lodging among them.

Psalm 55:15

I'm always amazed while reading the Psalms that David can move from quiet reflection on the beauty in nature to a frenzied tirade on his enemies. Until today—when I met the enemy.

It's winter. I'm delighted to be in our cozy mountain cabin, in my loft, at my desk, and feeling good. With only a short time to write before the demands of the day begin, I want to make tracks. Ideas are just jumping around in my head—far too many to contain in time and on paper. Today is a good time to let them fly.

Except for *the* fly—a large, obnoxious, black one with his incessant buzz so loud that I am unable to concentrate. He must have revived from winter slumber in the cabin's warmth. Just when there is a moment of silence, I relax and think him gone, but then he begins his frenzy again. Restless, aimless, confined as he is, I suppose he is as frustrated as I. He wants out but can't escape. I want him out but can neither catch him nor shoo him toward an open door or window. If we both want him to be free, why can't he be?

He doesn't know how he "bugs" me—he has no brain. I shouldn't let him bother me, but my brain attends to every sight and sound. The dilemma is troubling: The very things I need as a writer—attention to detail, the ability to notice things that others ignore, sensitivity, and awareness—just invite a lone fly to mess up a morning. Ideas, imagination, inspiration all fall on the waste pile at the sound and sight of one tiny monster of a fly.

The irony is that, come spring, I will carry his carcass, cremated by the heat, along with many other former buzzers in a dustpan outside and spread their remains to the winds. Fly, be fair—give up the ghost right now and shorten both of our misery. Stop your droning, and I will immortalize you on this page; if only you will end your infernal, repetitious noise and call it a day.

Bam—I may have gotten him—for one is trapped behind the blind. I raise it slowly with one hand and swat wildly with the other, just to be sure. The loud buzzing is muted. Now like David, I am free to sing—about "all creatures great and small." The enemy is vanquished. And immortal.

Dear God,

Help me rise above the irritations of life so I can rest in you. I will leave real vengeance in your hands. Amen.

Another World

As I walked through the parking lot and approached the building entrance, the clear air and the bright fall sky seemed to darken with each step I took. The small, ordinary building stood at one corner of a double chain-linked fence that surrounded a vast compound of weathered, graystone buildings. The two tall layers of coiled barbed wire on top of the fence sparkled menacingly.

To get from the building into the courtyard, I had to allow my bags to be inspected, my body searched by a metal detector; but, more importantly, my name had to be on a list, indicating that this visit was expected. Other visitors, probably friends and family, were searched more fully, asked to surrender their valuables and to pull their pockets inside out. Once declared "clean," we could be admitted and locked into a hallway between two sets of bolted doors. Finally the second lock clicked and a guard pushed open the last obstacle into the grounds of the Marysville prison for women.

Not wanting to stand out, I had worn a pair of beige slacks, a cotton shirt, and a sweater. When I finally met the women in the class that I was to observe, one of them smiled, pointing at my slacks. I looked around and discovered we were all wearing khaki—universal prison garb! Theirs were unstylish, standard issue and they wore solid color blouses of pink, green, rose, or black. I could have been a new inmate except for the color of my blouse. I soon learned that their "colors" were a symbol for the level of offense that brought them to this place.

The classroom building, the only new addition to the prison, was also standard issue—plain, undecorated walls, high ceilings and a long, narrow room with folding chairs in a ring pushed out to the walls. The women were already assembling, each with a notebook in hand. They were as curious about me as I was about them, and we acknowledged each other openly. Soon we were shaking hands and exchanging names as if arriving at a newcomers' club. The teacher properly introduced me, but my visitor status was immediately disregarded as the evening's work began.

The assignment that they brought with them to this class on communications was a letter written to someone on the outside. Part of the instruction, in addition to the proper form of a letter, was to describe just one event or topic and write as much detail as possible. They were to express their honest feelings toward the recipient of the letter. The letter was part of their encouragement to write, perhaps daily, in the spiral "journal" they were given at the beginning of the class a few weeks before.

Marge, who volunteered to be the first to read her letter aloud, walked to one end of the oblong ring of chairs, looking as confident as a corporate executive ready to make a presentation to the board. Thus began the round of recitations, with Marge tagging Juanita, who tapped the person she wanted to follow her. Each woman read with pride the words of her letter, using well formed sentences, descriptive words, and open emotion. Many letters were addressed to a mother or adult children who had tried to warn them about the men who led them astray. Letters, full of life and hope. More than once I had to blink back a tear.

For a few hours we were just women together, not divided by race or status or by our freedom or lack of it. I knew nothing of their crimes, nor they of *my* transgressions. Their letters expressed gentle love, anger and delight, sorrow and suffering. In their eloquent words I heard emotions and reflections like my own.

When the class time was over, I was reluctant to leave. I was given a reprieve when over the loudspeaker came a "squad" order, short for: Stay where you are until the emergency squad has checked the area. It gave us time for informal conversation. I was amazed at their forthrightness; they wanted me to know more about them than I felt free to ask. I didn't ask them how they got there, but they willingly revealed a range of offenses, the length of time they had served, and the time remaining on their sentences. A graying woman named Junella told me almost incidentally that black shirts like the one she wore indicated a murder conviction. Before I could react, the buzzer sounded. The stay order was lifted, and they were off like schoolgirls when the bell rings. I was left with only a bundle of impressions.

As I retraced my steps out of the series of locked doors and detectors and guards, I thought of the women I had left behind. Pretty, graceful, articulate, and bright are just a few adjectives that came to mind. Not until I reached my motel room, safely away from the prison walls, did I cry. I cried for my sisters behind the ugly wire of the compound. I cried for their mothers and children learning to live without them. I cried for a world in which evil is so strong and good often hard to find.

And I prayed that the hope and faith I witnessed among these extraordinary women would endure into their uncertain futures. I hoped against hope that each would get a chance to walk out of those doors—free from the walls, real and perceived, that limit them today.

Tips, Hints, and Advice

Ask yourself what distracts you most in your quest to become a writer? Motivation? Self doubt? Time commitments? If you can't beat 'em, write about 'em.

1. We introduce ourselves on the first day of class and tell why we signed up for the course. After one writer claims she has no interest in publication, many others echo the same anti-publication stance. One woman admits she would like to leave stories for her children and others nod their heads. A retired pastor says he is tired of being a public voice and longs for personal, private reflection. Betsy signed up for my follow-up course in which I urge them to make an outline or table of contents of the book in which their essays might reside. Betsy refused. To admit that her collected pieces of writing could become something frightened her. For years she'd been tucking her writing into greeting cards—publishing herself! Is it arrogant or faithful to seek an audience? Writing is God's gift. But, it also fits neatly under an overturned bushel basket. How do you plan to spread your words?

2. Hostages, POWs, inmates—I have often imagined their endless days. The stark surroundings I could endure. Even the lack of mobility and isolation from others. But having nothing to do might take away for me what it means to be human. I'd beg for two things—paper and a pencil. These are what keep me sane. Snippets of Bible verses and songs could be retrieved from memory and recorded for solace. Experience recalled and thoughts sorted, if only I could write. What would keep you sane if your freedoms were altered? Write about it.

3. I learned a lesson about hope in Africa. We traveled there from North America to understand something of the pandemic of AIDS.

The situation seemed hopeless to our Western minds: How could this virus be slowed, much less stopped, as it spread its death sentence into every town and the most distant villages? But we met hopeful people: relief staff working tirelessly on education and prevention, communities mobilizing to care for the children without parents, men and women with AIDS seeking ways to help others while they still felt well, and school children singing of their responsibilities to preserve Africa's future. I expected fatalism; I found hope. Many shared our ultimate hope of life with God after death. But their present hope was in living fully for as long as possible. Sharing with others in life brought the hope of caring by others in their dying. I want others to see this kind of hope—the kind of hope all of us need. I must write about it.

4. What distracts you most in your quest to become a writer? It could be motivation, self-doubt, subject choice, or time commitments. Or it could just be a flying insect that won't leave you alone. If you can't beat 'em, write about 'em. But don't let them drive you away from the page.

Writing Challenge

6

Think of a rare experience you have had that few people have ever experienced. Share the moment. Take everything in. Recreate the time, place, feelings, and wonder of it all through words.

Anne Dillard has brought me, through her writing, close to the natural wonders at Tinker Creek.[7] A friend tells and writes about being present when her daughter gave birth. I spent time in a women's maximum-security prison. Some of us have known times when we were "the only" in a group where every other person had an important feature in common.

Think of one such rare experience you have had that few people you know have ever experienced. Let us be there with you sharing the moment. Don't hurry the writing or the scene. Remember, we want to take everything in. We want to live vicariously through you. You will have to recreate the time, place, feelings, and wonder of it all through words.

Preachers often do this with biblical stories. In the hands of a good storyteller we can relive the event as if we were present. Some are concerned about the limits of imagination to "color" the text. Preacher and writer, Barbara Brown Taylor stresses "beholding" as well as believing in order to see "glimpses of truth" from God.[8] Our little stories seek no less.

Absence

Part of the inner world of everyone is this sense of emptiness, unease, incompleteness, and I believe that this in itself is a word from God, that this is the sound that God's voice makes in a world that has explained him away. In such a world, I suspect that maybe God speaks to us most clearly through his silence, his absence, so that we know him best through our missing him.

Frederick Buechner[1]

7

Blessed are those who hunger and thirst for righteousness, for they will be filled."[2] Restless people often hunger after something; a thing they cannot seem to find. The dis-ease shows itself in attempts to right wrongs or challenge oneself mentally or physically. A friend fears having empty time so much that she keeps a stack of novels handy to fill all spaces. Absence or emptiness is like a void that could suck her in.

Interruption of, or retirement from, regular work can create the same void. My father could not give up his job—partly fearing loss of meaning—until a heart attack took his life. Only when we lose something that has become fundamental to our lives and sense of well-being, do we

look into the emptiness. And then the pull, the longing, the lonesome-
ness can be our chance to recognize God's call.

Day Jobs

Come to me, all you who are weary and burdened, and I will give you rest.
Matthew 11:28

In 1993 I concluded that my day job could not support my writing habit. The management position at a public hospital consumed not only the nine-to-five hours but evenings and weekends as well. My expandable brown leather briefcase always bulged with writing projects that couldn't fit into busy, noisy days on the job. I began crossing boundaries into my personal time, those limits I so carefully held when the children lived at home. I worked day and night. Time for my own writing was relegated to the rare vacation or a Sunday afternoon when I refused to "work."

Every Sunday night, my husband noticed my tension rising as I anticipated the week's work ahead. I flew into my duties on Monday, almost feeling guilty for my Sabbath rest, and came home exhausted and discouraged. One day after one of many minor clashes with my boss, for whom no amount or quality of work was ever good enough, I announced I would resign. My husband could do nothing to dissuade me. He thought I should look for another day job before giving notice, but I was resolute. Now!

A spark of an idea to start my own business suddenly burst into flame. I would use my experience with grant proposal writing and become a contract technical writer. Because I had lots of professional contacts, it worked. A dream job come true! Independence, flexible time, good pay, and enormous satisfaction. Best of all, I was my own boss, working at home and filling any slack time with my own writing.

Two years later I ventured into the world of aspiring writers by attending the Iowa Summer Writing Festival in Iowa City. I took my fledgling pieces and shyly shared them with the twelve people in the group.

The other workshop members also had day jobs: two priests, a teacher, a member of a religious community, and so on. I shared my entrepreneurial work efforts. We also talked about freelancing and how little magazines were willing to pay for our labors. Suddenly someone asked, "Carol, how much do you charge for technical writing?" I was taken aback but answered honestly, "Sixty dollars per hour."

It wouldn't surprise me if some in that group decided to freelance with contract writing so that they, too, could feed themselves as well as their true passion to create.

Creator God,

Sometimes your calling to write has to be a sideline to making a living. Give me the patience to fashion my time so your first love for me also thrives. Amen.

A Light in the Window

My eyes stay open through the watches of the night, that I may meditate on your promises.

Psalm 119:148

Natalie Goldberg wrote *Wild Mind: Living the Writer's Life*[3] to assure fledgling writers that the nature of creativity is wild. The writer's mind never rests; it is always examining experiences, tying disparate pieces together, and creating something new. I often wonder if it is a blessing or a curse to live with a mental machine that runs night and day.

I used to chafe under such constant restlessness. To put that energy to use, I threw myself into causes: justice for the poor; early education for handicapped children; equal access for women, especially in the church. But even after progress on all fronts, the restlessness remains.

Writing has become my antidote. A spark here, a stray thought there, a sound or smell reminding me of past or future—and I run for the blank page. But even that is not enough. The restlessness wants to sort and find meaning—in short, to be nailed down in poems or essays or meditations.

My neighbors have commented on my study window, lighted well into the night. I'm a night person, especially when my husband is out of town. Sometimes, from the stillness and dark outside my window, a bit of wildness settles on the page. At times it even feels like light.

Meditation on God's promises can bring calm reassurance, but for me it also requires action. "Bind them [your commandments] on your fingers; write them on the tablet of your heart," the wise person penned in Proverbs (7:3). In the night I can't march or protest or even teach, but I can write. So I do.

Sometimes in morning light, the night inspiration looks like junk. Much too wild and rough on the edges. Time for left-brain revisions so that the written word can hope to see the light of day.

Thank you, God, for a restless mind. Help me harness its energy for you. Amen.

A Day in the Life ... and after

I'm quitting my job," I cried, as I rushed into his study and flopped down on the chair. "I can't stand to work there even one more day!" My husband was shocked at my words and my tears. Fritz didn't have to ask "Why?" for the word hung, unspoken in the room. I knew this would be the hardest part, just to explain myself and help him understand the depth of my feelings. On my long commute home from the office, I had asked myself all the questions. My answers were equivocal, but my resolve was not.

"I can't work for a person like her. Let me tell you what happened today ..." I proceeded to walk him through my first day back after a three-day vacation. She practically met me at the door and ordered me into her office. I made a quick detour to my desk to look over the mail and phone messages for clues, but there were none. When I entered her office, there were no preliminaries. She took out a legal pad and ticked off items one by one, demanding an update on each, some of minor importance and some from my quarterly goal sheet, still with plenty of time to complete. But as I tried to reply to each demand, she interrupted and went on. Her purpose was not to get answers, but to make a point: I was not productive enough to suit her, and today, now, and in this brash way, she meant to tell me so.

My work as research developer for the maternity and infant de-partment at a public hospital required skills different from those of clinic managers, whom my boss lifted up as models of production. If I were approaching three possible funders for a project, she wanted it to be five. If the due date for an application was still in the future, she wanted the approval and the money right then. When I completed a multi-year, complicated grant proposal and she signed off on it, she offered no words of thanks or approval, just reminded me that there was more of the same ahead and to get to work. She believed in the power of negative thinking.

Somehow, until this moment, I was able to take her for who she was, a young woman, talented enough to work her way into management and build her reputation around a tough, no-nonsense persona. She was fifteen years my junior and less educated than I. I never wanted her job, and she knew that. The pressure on her from those of higher rank I could only imagine, but I suddenly believed that *my* work was *her* "bottom line" for proving her right to the departmental leadership. Insecurity lurked under her facade of professionalism. I both feared and felt sorry for her, but for six years I had always tolerated her brusque manner in order to keep doing the work I loved. Until today. The thin straw just snapped. I knew right then, if I didn't leave I would regret it.

"I know this has been difficult," said Fritz as he put his hand over mine to stop the shaking, "but don't you want to find another job before leaving this one? You've worked so hard to get to this place in your career." So practical, so wise. But no, I could not. I was slipping into a place where I could no longer be honest with myself and accept her authority. I'll admit, I'm not a good fighter. The confrontational style, which my boss had perfected, made me want to run, not fight. For all my feminist verve, I had never learned to challenge unreasonable authority, especially from a woman who, all my instincts told me, was really on my side.

There followed a night of self-doubting, sleepless meandering of my mind. Was I so weak that her words wilted me? Couldn't I just reassure her that I was working on everything we set out to do, humor her, knowing tomorrow that her harangues would be directed at someone else in the department? Was I really willing to sacrifice a good job for an unknown future? I reminded myself that I had never enjoyed working under someone, always chafing in one way or another. Perhaps that was my ultimate work flaw: thinly veiled insubordination.

In the morning, nothing had changed. I wrote out my letter of resignation. I would have to do this one alone. Whether or not anyone else understood, I finally did. My daughter Sue might. Maybe it was her words, spoken while we walked together the previous week, that brought me to this point. We were sharing our "work woes." As a grade-school art teacher, she is burdened by the pettiness among teachers, parents, and administrators until she has to unload it. Over more than a year, my troubles had not changed; still the same as they were that day. She listened and clarified my words again in her mind, and suddenly blurted,

"Mom, I don't want to be mean, but I'm so sick of hearing about your boss. Let's talk later when you decide to do something about it."

Until I decide—how right she was! The aggravations at work came from outside, but since I could not control the maverick making the decisions, I had to make a choice. Take her abuse or go, not unlike many women faced with domineering or cruel husbands. But where was my shelter, my safe-space? There would be so much explaining to do. Was it really *that* bad? Could I just walk away from this security and source of so much professional satisfaction?

The boss showed no shock when she opened the envelope and read. She did not try to talk me out of going. Others were incredulous. Why? By then my answer was ready, even as an alternate plan was forming. "I'm going into business for myself," I said with as much confidence as I could muster. "I've decided to do the same proposal-writing work but independently of the hospital." I mentioned only to trusted colleagues that leaving was a matter of survival. They had all considered the same move but for personal reasons didn't dare to defy or leave.

The day after I hit work's rock bottom was the most creative day of my life. All the energy I had used to fume and fret came rushing out to fill the void and become a business plan for working and living a better way. I would work out of my home office, offer my services to people who would really appreciate what I could do for them, and control both my time and my work environment.

Today, I sit at my computer, writing with enthusiasm. I'm dressed in sweats and sneakers with my Diet Coke on my desk. I'm busy. I smile to recall that the first three contracts in my new technical writing business five years ago were from my former, nettlesome boss. Evidently she valued my work enough to hire me at a hefty consulting fee to complete them. Now I know that others do, too. And finally—I've found a boss I can work for.

Tips, Hints, and Advice

Writers need to be self-directed, otherwise no copy will be written. That trait often makes working "for" other people difficult.

1. Everything I know about Zen Buddhism, I learned from Natalie Goldberg—writing guru and practicing Buddhist. The object of "sitting" in meditation is to empty one's mind. Long sessions of nothingness are thought to benefit creativity. It must be like a vacuum. The mind is temporarily cleared of all rational thought so that, at a certain point, new thoughts rush in to fill the void. The closest I've come is while driving long distances on an interstate highway where objects or scenery to distract you are few. I've had great moments while taking my turn at driving a car full of sleeping family across the Great Plains toward Colorado. The all-night talk radio is my only companion until I turn it off. In the nothingness, thoughts climb aboard and keep me awake with their surprises. What do you do when you cannot "do?" Plan for the next time you hold a pen.

2. So often I stop myself in the middle of something mundane and wonder what distinguishes the ordinary moments we forget from the special ones we remember. During the pause, if I look around at the detail of the task or the object or the words on a page, the moment becomes extraordinary. Reflection on the ordinary is one way to examine the void. Like going from black-and-white to color, a new dimension appears. Visual artists do it all the time; language artists can, too.

3. Writers need to be self-directed; otherwise no copy will be written. That trait often makes working "for" other people difficult. Bosses rarely honor self-starters by letting them manage their work and their time. If you are a doer who needs

no direction, get yourself free to write. You have a different calling. Some would say it's a "higher" calling.

4. My late mother lived in a Christian retirement center the last three years of her life. An avid reader, she regularly used the library, which containined predominantly Christian books. She often lamented that all the stories came out rosy: "That's not the way my life has been. The stories don't seem true." She would agree with Frederick Buechner who urges novelists, in particular, to tell not only about times that "glimmer with God's presence," but those days when God seems absent, as well.

5. Perhaps sermons are somewhat formulaic. In that way, they are closer to technical than creative writing. Many preachers were taught to develop a sermon like an essay—usually with three points, bounded by an introduction and a conclusion. The latter was designed to be what listeners took away with them. Forget form in the first draft of creative writing. E.M. Forster said, "Only connect."[4] Begin by drawing the reader into the dilemma, the strange happening, or the irony. Once you have his attention carry him along with you during exploration. The journey will be more satisfying for both of you. Not a bad idea for a sermon, either.

Writing Challenge

7

Think of a time when either a planned or an unexpected change left you feeling disoriented or alone. Write your story of such an event.

Think of a time when either a planned or an unexpected change left you feeling disoriented or alone. Gone were the very things that you had always taken for granted. My sudden decision to leave a long-held and mostly satisfying job left me with a void that had to be filled. The next day became the most creative day of my life.

Perhaps you have experienced a similar loss or void. What happened right afterward? How did the experience change your life? All "change events" require a response from you. Were you aware of divine direction in your reaction and subsequent action?

Write your story of such an event. Maybe your response was sudden, almost intuitive or it may be continually unfolding. Let the reader experience your upheaval following a life-changing event.

Labors

Holiness and craft come together at this point; the moment of the poem is also the moment of salvation. Both occur in the present. I make my way as a poet and as a Christian by giving my attention to being in Christ, and in doing in Him the work before me. Quoting Thomas Merton, "It is in the ordinary duties and labors of life that the Christian can and should develop his spiritual union with God."

John Leax[1]

8

Worthy causes have driven my work life. A need greater than my own always sparked energy for change; the way things were was not the way they had to be. Idealism, imagination, restlessness, optimism—all of these drove me. But jobs, those bundles of day-to-day hard work, were never ideal or always upbeat. People and priorities and just the volume of responsibility often tarnished the worthiest of causes.

My first glimpse of that spiritual union with God as coworker came through writing. The union, Merton wrote,[2] unites the worker and her maker around the work itself. God cares about the ordinary—the humdrum as well as flashes of insight—and invites us to join him in common places. My restlessness doesn't disappear; there is work to do. But, the Holy Spirit energizes *my* spirit to persevere to the end of each task and to the end of this life.

Writing in the Din

Go now, write it on a tablet for them, inscribe it on a scroll, that for the days to come it may be an everlasting witness.

Isaiah 30:8

The culmination of my graduate work was to do original research on a subject of societal concern. I designed a study of parents of low-birthweight babies during the era of the so-called Baby Doe Regulations[3]—rules imposed on physicians regarding medical intervention with very small and fragile infants. The study grew as the result of interaction with parents in the neonatal intensive care unit during a nine-month period.

The contacts with parents usually occurred as I observed their infant in the Plexiglas Isolette, read the monitors, and listened to medical personnel confer about treatment. Tensions were sky high. Thoughts were expressed incoherently, incompletely. But my job as witness was to capture those expressions.

After each contact with a parent, I'd hurry to the hospital cafeteria and scrawl my "field notes" amid the din of hundreds of voices. I've never been good at coping with noise when trying to think, but somehow in the urgency to be true to the parents, I willed my pen to do its work in spite of the noise. The notes filled many pages and became "data" for my dissertation. In my field this is called ethnography, a scientific description of a culture—in this case the culture of parents within a lifesaving unit for infants.

I can't bear to throw away my handwritten field notes. They are reminders that experiences not recorded quickly lose some of their emotional potency. Field notes are rough. They don't resemble the final, polished prose that is publishable, but they contain emotional truth that can form the basis of even formal, "scientific" writing.

Ever since that time in my life, I carry a small notebook and make field notes of real life as I experience it. Words hastily jotted in a noisy café will one day bring energy to my writing. Together they will have the permanent power to witness.

Dear God,

Thank you for prizing the written word, both the quick notes and the scrolls for posterity. Give me eyes and ears that are open to your truth. Amen.

Miraculous Cleanup

I am the vine; you are the branches. When you're joined with me and I with you, the relation intimate and organic, the harvest is sure to be abundant. Separated, you can't produce a thing.

John 15:5, *The Message*

There they were, scattered on my kitchen table—hundreds of pieces of "data" on small squares of paper. For the first time since starting the study of parents of low-birthweight infants, I panicked. Why hadn't I chosen a quantitative study in which the data collected would be numerical, so much easier to use as statistical proof of my hypothesis? I had been warned: Qualitative studies may be interesting (mine certainly was), but writing the results takes more time and ingenuity.

Little did I realize until I looked at all the snippets of paper how difficult my job would be. Morning after morning I shuffled the papers, tried to create categories, and searched for some sort of an organizational scheme. Each day a new configuration, but no clear direction. Inevitably the day passed until the table was needed for supper. My tension rose as precious time passed and I saw no clear way to interpret and report the data.

One morning I sat with head in hands—close to despair. I turned my troubled thoughts into a prayer: "God, I just can't do this thing. I have tried so hard and long but I just don't see my way." It was a primitive cry for help. But it was more. With sudden clarity I knew I could not do this, the biggest intellectual challenge of my life, without God's help. There I was, sitting with my hands opened upward, asking to be filled.

I'll admit I'm usually skeptical about divine intervention, especially when it comes to schoolwork. Did I think God would just bail me out when I wasn't up to the task? I grew up thinking God handed out talents, but the applied stuff was up to the people he entrusted with the treasure.

What happened was nothing short of miraculous. The pieces started to make sense just as in a crossword puzzle when a key word is found.

Before my family gathered for the evening meal, I had completed an outline and organized the field notes into numerous envelopes for the sections! The breakthrough came when I finally moved aside and asked God to break *into* every part of my life and work.

Dear God,

You came just in time. From now on, I'll remember to acknowledge you in all my ways, the path you promised to direct. Amen.

First Things First

First: in line, to be chosen, top priority, the best, the beginning, top quality, the leader, first-born, numero uno. "So the last will be first, and the first will be last."

Matthew 20:16

Every morning from those early stirrings in bed of sluggish body and scattered mind, I must make some choices. What first? What next? My winter days begin by donning a jacket over PJs and robe, slipping into heavy socks and boots and taking Jake, our black lab out for a walk. Out here in the country, it's not necessary to go with him—a quick whistle or the word "biscuit" will bring him back. But I like to feel the day firsthand before I plunge into it. If we are up "on time" (my husband's euphemism for early), it is still dark. The silhouettes of bare trees in the bordering woods come into focus, especially under some moon glow. Jake and I come in when the cold nips my scantily covered legs.

My work calls as I sip morning tea, then shower and make the bed. Always the nagging question, "What first?" After all these necessary firsts, what agenda will I choose? It is amazing how many of the things I do want to be first: the journal, exercise, meditation, that mental essay that needs to take on life in words, quick calls to family, the meeting minutes that should have been done yesterday, the e-mail that might affect the course of the day.

While in grad school I read a paper entitled "Decidophopia." The article wasn't as informative as the one-word title. As I face this desk each day, I know I've got it. I must decide, but I am afraid. To make one thing first pushes everything else lower on the list. My desk is usually covered with notebooks and loose paper in stacks—each one a "should." On a casual sweeping glance, little flares seem to go up like hands of school children who know the answer: "Me!" "Me!" "Me!"

At standard jobs, some decisions aren't in a worker's control. Several times my choices were preempted by a note from my boss on my desk that read: "Come to see me right away." A visit to the coffee machine in any office shows how many others are facing the same dilemma: where to start.

Two prolific writers seem to have good ideas. Joseph Epstein writes in the January, 2002, issue of *Atlantic Monthly* about 5:00 a.m. appointments at his kitchen table to write before anything else vies for his attention.[4] Hemingway is said to have always stopped a writing session in the middle of a scene or thought so that, the first thing the next day, he'd have to finish and go on. But, I'm a night person, and my conscience won't let me sleep until the task is complete.

So, each morning, I'll just follow my whims this way and that until I discover a flare bright enough to choose as today's first, knowing it won't be the last.

Dear God,

Thanks for the many challenges you put before me. Give me wisdom for making some firsts. Amen.

The Touch of the Personal Essay

The trick is to realize that one is not important, except insofar as one's example can serve to elucidate a more widespread human trait and make readers feel a little less lonely and freakish.

Phillip Lopate, *The Art of the Personal Essay*[5]

I write for a living—your basic writer-for-hire, tackling the jobs that people cannot do or do not want to sweat over. At times my hired words describe the plight of persons or neighborhoods or cities in trouble, and then propose a plan to combat the problem. If I do it well, using every shred of important information persuasively, the reviewer may perceive the need as if it were his own and award my client the funds to create a social program. It is honest work that I enjoy, but it is only a day job for someone like me, restless to write about the subject I know best—myself.

"My little stories," I used to call them. I would pour them out on paper, more to make sense of what was happening in and around me than to tell them to anyone. But as I thought about letting the writing see the light of day, I judged the words before the ink dried, with the uncompromising standards of a veteran English teacher, and relegated them to the bottom drawer. But I never cleaned the drawer; I could not part with one word that came from my hand. Over the years the scraps of paper and every manner of notebook piled up. I was beginning to understand the drive to write, which the poet Rilke characterized as "a small voice calling in the night."[6] The voice or choirs of voices would not give me any peace.

Like most writers who are not schooled in the art, I had no idea what form my writing would or should take. I doubted my imaginative powers for real fictional storytelling, and I knew I couldn't tell a joke to save myself. I liked the sounds of words and the music they evoked but also had no idea how to fashion a poem. In the end I could only define my writing by what it was not: nonfiction.

When I first began to write "pieces" with a beginning and an end and some sort of point, I opted for a short form, meditations of about 400 words each. It was my mother's suggestion and a good way to start, but when I shared them with other writers, they asked for more. It seemed that each topic had a complexity that begged for further development. My barebones ideas teased the reader, and I soon came to realize that the moral lessons they taught were forced. I still wanted to say the same things, but with the voice of a prophet, not a preacher. More like Isaiah, who created beautiful sensory pictures, "the voice of one crying in the wilderness," and "all we like sheep have gone astray."

In the same way I am drawn to the images used by the Old Testament prophet, I am drawn to his intimate style. Perhaps I write because I just want to talk with someone, for I always imagine a person listening to my words, even as I write them in the quiet of my study. And this unseen listener and I, we laugh over the quirks of both my writing and my life; but as readily we cry together at stories of heartbreak. As with a friend, nothing is too insignificant to share. My imagined reader seems eager to know what makes me tick as well as what keeps me going when life's worst fears come to my door.

I am neither famous nor heroic, so I do not presume to write an autobiography or a memoir of my entire life. Neither does my mind make a straight line from A to B, forming a chronology. Sometimes small clips of life come in sequence, but for the most part they are just little impressions that seem ironic or noteworthy when a spark connects them. Memories hit me at their time, not mine, and compel me to sketch them out in story. Like the time I watched three kids waiting for their grandmother to arrive at an airport. Suddenly their anticipation and expectation were my own, as if *I* were expecting someone I loved.

The package for my writing is the personal essay—that wonderfully open and intimate form that allows me total freedom within a writing structure. I lack the cleverness to disguise my words by putting them into someone else's mouth, so I own up to them right away. As peculiar as they are, the actions are mine alone. The essay lets me display my foibles, with self-conscious grace.

The personal essay for me needs a subtle form, like a little thread woven through that holds the piece together and brings it unity and completeness—a sense of movement and direction but within some sort of a frame. But as I move along in this chosen form of writing I become aware that I gravitate toward a lightness of tone and plain language that bring out, much like poetry, the feelings that led me to the page to tell the story. For me, the essay provides an ideal format, one that encourages me to fill a few pages with ideas around a topic or an event or a growing feeling in my soul.

And so I moonlight nights and weekends by writing personal essays—about myself. "I" am the voice telling the story or feeling the harsh wind or crying over a lost love. But somehow, if the essay springs as much from my heart as my head, it may touch the "I" of some readers and become their story, too. Perhaps that is what de Montaigne meant when he said, "Every man has within himself the entire human condition."[7] My unique experience, told in my own words, somehow binds me to others as it links us in common humanity.

I confess that even as those voices inside beg to be heard, I work to calm my fears. I don't like to fail. It would be much easier not to have written at all, except for this unrelenting pressure to tell my story. The worst thing about stories is they must be told to someone. The drawer is getting full. I need to make a choice: get buried in the scrap heap or publish. Only then will I know if the reader I imagine is really listening.

**Tips,
Hints,
and
Advice**

*I think of
words as an
offering—an
everyday gift
to my maker.*

1. The first part of writing is fun; I played at it for a long time. The end of writing, just before other eyes beside my own see it, is hard work. Another standard is imposed on my play. Left-brain analysis replaces right-brain, nondirected reflection.
   - Are my ideas clearly stated?
   - Are there too many or too few metaphors and do they get along?
   - Are all nouns specific and adjectives vivid?
   - Is tense consistent?
   - Do my subjects and verbs agree?
   - Is there tension and resolution?

   Take a page of your writing and read it one time for each criterion. Change the words for the better.

2. Poet Patricia Clark tells a small, poetry loving group her four S's of poetry: *sensory, specific, sentiment* and *sparkling language*. And, just for good measure, adds *tension* and *compression*. "Poems are short; every word counts," she says. And then she sends us off to write a verse.[8] It is hard to feel free with six "shoulds" hanging over your head. Good advice to save for rewrite time. By then I'll know what I wanted to say.

3. "Being in Christ, and doing in Him the work before me." John Leax[9] has a strong sense of belonging. That security gives him license to write as his calling, which brings him close to God. When I am tempted to ask the question, "What is all this worth?" I beg for that close-knit surety. I think of words as an offering—an everyday gift to my maker.

4. Since I gave up my technical writing business, my right brain is taking over. That's good for creative writing, but bad for keeping my desk clean, remembering dates, organizing submissions, knowing which draft of a piece of writing is the most recent, and just moving from task A to task B to task C. My goal was to write in the morning and do office work in the afternoon, but when I'm at my desk, I'd rather write. I envy these quick switchers: writing poetry one minute and computer troubleshooting the next. Perhaps I'll have to alternate the days: left brain on Tuesday, Thursday, and Saturday; right brain Monday, Wednesday, and Friday. At least I won't cross the wires and risk a power outage.

5. Lists are a good way to compress lots of information into a little package. They can be packed with meaning and images that can serve as shorthand for narrative. An excerpt from *The Things They Carried*, by Tim O' Brien,[10] impressed me. Like most writers, I responded to the tragedy of September 11, 2001 in my own way. I wrote two long lists, packed into configurations of The World Trade Center's demolished twin towers. The writing began as an a-b-c drill in which I imagined all the things and all the ideas that remained trapped forever in the collapsed, compressed twin towers. Most of your lists won't be 800 items long.

Using all the letters of the alphabet, pose a question to yourself, such as "What have I outgrown?" or "What would I grab if my house were on fire?" Write them out. Use the list as subject matter or as a way to record many things without slowing down your story.

Writing Challenge

8

Write about the hardest job you have ever done in your life. What perspective did it give to your life-work?

Consider Donald Hall's famous opening line in *Life Work*: "I never worked a day in my life."[11] He makes his point by comparing the toil of his ancestors with his life as a poet. My father-in-law, a foundry worker, would have agreed. Two of his four sons made careers as postal workers; now that was work. The other two, by contrast, "taught." What do reading, talking, and writing have to do with "labor?" Teaching doesn't even make you sweat or get your hands dirty!

But Donald Hall went on to describe his work habits. He writes every day, beginning with revisions of poems in progress. He reconsiders each word and phrase and inks in the changes. Later in the day, old and revised poems along with new ones go to his typist. She returns the new draft, along with the numbered old draft. Donald says he sometimes nears one hundred drafts before he gets it right. His standards for good work are high.

Think about how you work at writing. If you are just beginning, form a work plan; it can always be revised as you move forward. Unlike manual labor, there is no right or preferred way to do it. It would be difficult to learn from another writer "on the job" as is so common in apprentice situations. Write about the hardest job (other than writing) you have ever done in your life. What perspective did it give to work?—to *your* life-work?

Fervor

J. D. Salinger's famous line, "It's not over till the fat lady sings," never held any mystery for me. Writer to writer, Salinger was planting a seed of crazy belief at the turn of the '60s that has since spread into an impenetrable thicket of faith, as long as those little black marks are marching across white pages somewhere—in a drawer, in a trunk, in an attic—the possibility remains that they will ultimately find their audience.

You can slip paper clips under the nails of the hundreds of thousands of aspiring writers, wannabe writers, grimly determined journeyman writers, and writers attempting to match or exceed an early success, and you'll never wipe out that faith. It's as tough, in the face of punishment, as religious fervor.

Suzanne Lipsett[1]

9

I read many books about writing. Sometimes one word seems to jump from the page. Suzanne Lipsett's use of that little word "fervor" in *Surviving the Writing Life* attracted my attention. Combining it with "religious" is almost a cliché, but perhaps belief is fuel so powerful that it can overcome all sorts of things that contradict or negate it. New believers and new writers have something in common: fervor.

My husband met a new Christian who came to faith, not by family or evangelism but by reading the Bible, cover to cover, several times. His fervor spilled everywhere; he marveled that anyone could take God's extraordinary message for granted. Writers are often filled with other kinds of fervor: eagerness, passion, gusto, love, enthusiasm, relish, and fire. Obstacles appear to dampen the writing life, but all that fervor can crash right through barriers. Most of us have never been persecuted because of our faith or our writing. We'll count on fervor in the face of persecution.

Sensations

The ideal view for daily writing, hour on hour, is the blank wall of a cold-storage warehouse. Failing this, a stretch of sky will do, cloudless, if possible.

Edna Ferber[2]

There are days when I seriously wonder if I should be a writer. Not only does noise distract me—sights and smells and motion and touch do, as well. Visual distraction may be the worst, or at least right up there with sound. I've heard writers exude praises for writing in cafés, but I prefer an environment free of distractions.

In my study the desk faces the interior of the room, so my back borders the window. Sometimes I reward myself for a good session with time to gaze over the landscape and the sky, but I must put it behind me to work. Most of my books are outside the room in a hall library, or they would constantly tempt me with their treasures. I write by hand, so my eyes are perpetually focused on the blank sheet filling with bold letters. It might be more efficient to compose my work on screen, but then I'd let computer noise and motion in the door. My pen must roll without hesitation across the page, which means I pick pens and paper very carefully. When my fluorescent light began flickering recently, I wasted no time getting a new bulb.

Our breadmaker gets used almost every day. As it reaches the baking cycle in the kitchen below, I shut my door so that the wonderful smell stays put. Even when writing a series of meditations on clouds, I'm off on tangents if I catch sight of one.

Many days I question my choice of vocation. With so many quirks and idiosyncrasies that hamper, why do I try? Or, short of giving it up, why not find a stark, cold-storage room without windows? Or a spare cabin in the woods like the one that was Annie Dillard's home for work?[3]

I'm fortunate. I have a study in a quiet corner of the house, and I know how to find remote carrels in most libraries. When my surroundings cannot be controlled, I do the writer's other work: collecting sights and sounds, the motion of happy children and nature's notes. My mental storehouse sorts and compacts the incoming data and will let me draw from its bins when my spirit is blessed with the absence of all things sensory.

Dear God,

You provide all I need to keep going. Sustaining me to create—what a blessing! Amen.

Preach It, Brother

If you want to write for religious publications, you must be especially careful not to start sermonizing, offering "testimony" or using religious buzzwords. People want stories, not sermons.

Mary Ann O'Roark[4]

Reviewing the writer's guidelines from Christian publishers, I notice one common theme: "Don't be preachy!" This warning comes from people within the faith. I wonder if writing, even about religious and spiritual themes, should be distinct from "preaching" the same message. My dictionary gives a clue in its definition of preachy: "tediously or pretentiously didactic." So, both sermons and writing can be "preachy"—trying to pound a point instead of proclaiming the good news and trusting the hearer to personalize the message and make it her own.

I grew up in more formal times when the preacher was called "Dominee." He was often the only well educated person in the community and carried an air of superiority. Even his voice changed when he spoke from the pulpit; *Preekje*, it is called in Dutch. Today ministers often adopt a more conversational tone in preaching, emphasizing the shepherd's, or servant's role, rather than the one of being "in charge" of a church.

A different standard for preaching applied within the multiracial congregation of which I was a member. When the sermon pitch rose to its "preachiest," voices would call out, "Preach it, Brother!" and "Amen!" The preacher increased the volume because he had connected with the audience in dialogue, a sure sign they were listening. At that point the words "preached" were less important than the words "felt."

Undoubtedly, hearing adds meaning to the written word. In my writers' group, members read their work aloud, usually with expression and emphasis on the important words. A better test of a piece of writing—which must stand alone in black-and-white when published—is hearing it in your mind. The words alone must give meaning: inspiration instead of orders.

Good writing about spiritual matters, the experts say, cannot tell what the reader is supposed to see. Words alone will have to draw the scene, the characters, and the action. Effective religious writing can be as inspirational as the Word itself.

Dear God,

Help us share your deepest truths, as we know them, in words that show wonder and delight. Amen.

One Little Spud

And God said, "Let the land produce living creatures according to their kinds"…
Then God said, "Let us make man in our image … in our likeness"
Genesis 1:24a, 26a

If you want to feel like just one little potato in a semitrailer full of them, go to a writers' conference. As eager as I am each year to spend a week in Iowa, the first meeting of all the participants at the Summer Writing Festival in a large banquet hall has a sobering effect. Our numbers are legion, and we represent only one of many groups. The same size crowd appears each week and weekend during the summer, here and in numerous other locations.

Each year, I become part of a small group of writers who concentrate intensely together on our craft and seek the opinion of each other about whether a piece of writing "works." We are always aware of the multitudes like ourselves who want to write *and* publish. We are smart enough to know the odds. Little potatoes? Sure, but we know we are with our own kind.

Like most writers, I am first of all a reader. My children, now grown, know I'll find a library in every new town I move to before I locate the grocery store. Words are my food; making word combinations is like cooking a complex meal without a recipe.

I once spent time in a bibliotech in Amsterdam. Except for some English periodicals, most of the books were in a language I could not read. It didn't matter. I was in the company of books. Their potential was unbounded as was mine, that day, as a writer.

Talk about potential. To be an image-bearer, yes, *like God*, puts me in company with the divine. As much as I look a lot like every other "spud," I have a mark on me. I have work to do.

"We like each other's company," a classmate said over dinner after an Iowa class. To be in the company of good books and earnest writers fills me up—for a while. Then I must feed the muse. I will starve if reading, writing, and prayer are not everyday meals.

Dear God,

You made me like you, and you feed me everyday. Being in company with you fills me with all that I need. Amen.

Retirement Writing

It means for us simply that we must be careful with our lives, for Christ's sake, because it would seem that they are the only lives we are going to have in this puzzling and perilous world, and so they are very precious and what we do with them matters enormously.

Frederick Buechner[5]

I've decided to write for the rest of my life!" I declare to those people I care about who will be affected by my plans. I'm ready to make a lifelong commitment to something that was until now only a hobby, a sideline. Some who hear the news don't take it seriously. "Just humor her," they may be thinking. "She'll get distracted, she always does." But all the people in my circle calculate, just in case it might be true, how my decision will affect them.

We mothers and grandmothers tend to be hubs of interwoven activities. We keep everything together for good times and holidays; let's face it—we make things happen. I wonder if they are wondering, "If Mom has a higher goal, we might not be able to count on her. What does she mean, to write? Dabble? Doodle? Or really drive to accomplish? If she is serious, maybe she won't be there when we need child care or a holiday gathering place or a listening ear."

I sense their disbelief that I really want to hole up in my study away from real life and just write about it. In the middle of their most intense years of family, the whole enterprise of writing seems like an indulgence of someone who hasn't enough real work to do. They may not understand. I'll have to live with that.

But I am concerned about the implications of "the rest of my life." During the years after my mother moved from Colorado into a nearby retirement home, I faced aging through her experience. She lived to be ninety two, always enthusiastic about living, but not afraid to die. She was twenty-seven when I was born, so unconsciously I gauge my life by hers. But long life is never assured, and she reminded me that systems begin to fail. Will the mind, hand, and keyboard still produce words up until my end? Will I even make it to such ripeness of age? And more troubling: Her life has been one built on helping others. Will writing help anyone? I can't judge the worth of my own writing to others, but the writing of others daily inspires me.

My goal—however bold it sounds—is not specific. Perhaps it isn't a goal at all, just a statement of intent. There are no predictions about pages per day or publication, and certainly not about excellence. But I told a friend just yesterday, "My decision to write in retirement has been the most freeing of my life. I never wonder how I will spend my days." So liberating, challenging, invigorating! Full of possibilities until the end. Someday my family will understand.

Dear God,

I pray for a long life—of writing. May the passion never wane, for Christ's sake. Amen.

Legacy

It's time to read bedtime stories to the four-year-old cousins who are having a sleepover, which happens to coincide with my visit. I'm eager for the two little guys to snuggle up to me and get their nightly dose of imagination. Each can choose one book, I say in my grandmotherly way, and they race off to the bulging bookcase to make a selection. I'm pleased when Matt chooses the western spoof of *Cinderella* that I bought for him last Christmas.

But just as we are ready for the fun part, nine-year-old Lindsay appears and asks, "Can I read the books to them?" I reluctantly defer, and she begins the tale of Miss Lurleen and Cowboy Slim, the Cinderella/ Prince counterparts. In a flawless Western twang, she reads page after page, and the boisterous boys melt at the sound of her voice reading the story they have heard many times before.

My daughter and I look on from a distance. I don't know which of us is more fascinated by the girl in the middle.

"The first time I read the book, I read it like that, but couldn't always remember to keep up the accent," says Barb. "Lindsay took the clue from me but has perfected it." Then she tells me that her daughter's fifth grade teacher, Mr. Smith, is working on reading with expression and has asked her to read aloud as an example to her class.

"Lindsay learned to read from you, and she has never read without gusto," Barb tells me. "Those words just come to life." The boys on the sofa are spellbound.

I am in awe of this child. I sometimes tease her that she taught me how to be a grandmother since she knew I never knew my grandmothers. Lindsay and I had been learning together for five years before Matt and Chris became rivals for a place on my lap. What fun to learn from Lindsay, who excelled in language from an early age. She loved to talk and sing and rhyme words and listen to stories and write the alphabet. On their twenty-five minute commute to work and day care, she and her mom spent most of it in word play over the lively pop music on the radio.

Lindsay and I are together frequently despite the five-hour drive that separates us. In addition to the weekend visits, she has spent at least a week alone at my house once each year, and we often take vacations together in the mountains. Her reading just erupted one day when she was four, so I don't take credit for teaching her. Lindsay has always loved jigsaw puzzles, and for her reading was like a giant puzzle. She reveled in decoding all those squiggles on the page and finding out they had meaning. One of our first reading lessons took place in church, where we were supposed to be quiet. I'd show her a word such as *God* on a page in the Bible and ask her to find more of that word. The words must have stood upright on the page for her, because she found them all.

Good times for us have always revolved around reading, telling stories, and writing them. She used to sit on my lap at the computer, poking out the letters to spell the words for a little story. When she grew tired, she agreed to dictate to me. As a novice grandmother, I marveled at each step in her understanding. We collected her writing in a notebook.

Had my own preschool children similarly impressed me at this age? I recollect some of the awe with our first child, Lindsay's mother. Barb talked readily, by the age of two could easily name all the tropical fish in our aquarium, and insisted, "I can do it myself." With all our three children, I read stories aloud while sitting on the long, Danish-modern sofa. That was our marker of a day well spent. I hardly noticed when the youngest began to read on her own, before starting school. Perhaps she was impatient from having to wait for her story time. Now, I would certainly notice an early reader amoung my grandchildren.

I recall almost nothing of my own discovery of the written word. I have very little memory of life before the age of ten. I'm sure I learned to read in the first grade with Miss Vanden Hoek, but I have no mental records of joy or accomplishment. My sister, two years older, often read to me, and it may have been her oral reading that etched itself into my subconscious. As I watch Lindsay reading to the boys, something stirs from the past.

Lindsay and I have a new game: the writing challenge. I showed her some of the techniques I learned in writing classes: the cluster, the freewrite, and alphabet/word recall. We decide on an assignment, write side-by-side, and then read the results to each other. Since she is just beginning to write "reports" for school, she loves to assume the role of teacher and assign me a task: to write on a topic of her choosing. Last time my word was "starvation" picked at random from the dictionary. Hers was "kangaroo," a topic she'd done some research about. After about fifteen minutes I told her to assign me another word because this one made me too sad. Our word play continued for hours until the kitchen table was needed for other things.

Tonight the reader and the listeners have gone to bed, dreaming, I suppose, about the world of possibilities that comes to life with words in books. Barb and I talk on, each with a book in hand. She tells me of her recent parent-teacher conference at school, in which the teacher told Barb what happened when she gave Lindsay a compliment about a story she was writing: "You write very well." Her immediate answer: "I get it from my grandmother; she's a writer." I laugh. It doesn't take much to impress a grandchild.

Really, Lindsay Jo—I'm sixty years old and have just begun to express myself through writing. At not-quite-ten, you have already been part of my writing education and often its theme. I believe you have already surpassed your teacher. But no matter who is teaching whom, the love of writing and each other is what binds us.

**Tips,
Hints,
and
Advice**

*Throw
yourself into
writing about
something
you love,
or fear, or
loathe—and
feel the fervor.*

1. Call it religious fervor; call it writing fervor. Suzanne Lipsett says it's the same tough stuff. I like this word that conjures warmth, earnestness, and intensity. It reminds me of the best writing sessions, those filled with a strong but welcoming heat. Maybe even light, like the flame of a log in the woodburning stove when the door is opened just a little. Throw yourself into writing about something you love, or fear, or loathe—and feel the fervor.

2. All writing requires research unless the writer knows everything. My husband is a naturalist, so often I lean on him for answers about little creatures or plants or trees. But if I ask much beyond name and habitat, he often admits he doesn't know. For example, we had a five-day ice storm this spring, but on the day the ice melted the frogs began their cheeping. I imagined they were frozen in the bog. Writing about nature takes more than awe or fervor to get the facts correct. I'll have to do some research on that one.

3. The hottest kind of religious fervor arises from controversy. Are not words such as *infidel, pagan, crusade* and *jihad* born out of the clash of beliefs? Firmly held notions can become the cause for war and even bloodshed. Understanding fervor may be the first step toward the meeting of unlike minds. Fervor can prompt strong writing. Writing out the passion may avert bloody clashes.

4. Some readers of this book may take exception to the warning against preaching in your writing aimed for a Christian audience. I, and most publishers of books that appeal to Christians, believe that bad writing cannot be camouflaged

behind pious phrases. Words of faith are becoming a cliché. Faith talk has been used so often we think the meaning is clear. Try a fresh approach for your deepest feelings about God. In the style of Eugene Petersen in *The Message*, rewrite any Psalm in a way your 15-year-old neighbor would understand. Guard the message; proclaim today's truth.

5. "Why don't more pastors become writers?" I asked a friend in the clergy as he delivered his meditations for publication. I reason that, if I wrote one or two sermons a week, I'd be filling books in no time at all. He explained, "Writing sermons for presentation is different—what the words don't carry your gestures, expressions, tone, and volume, will." Most sermons don't come across well on the flat page. The listener (reader) is faceless. The context of the worshipper or the congregation is unknown. The words must carry all the weight of communication. Compare a sermon of yours with one of Barbara Brown Taylor or Frederick Buechner. Note the difference in fervor.

Writing Challenge

9

Make two lists: one about things you love and the other about things you hate or despise. Choose what brings out your most powerful response and write fervently about it today.

Remember the last time you completed a questionnaire or opinion poll? You were given a list of statements to react to with five choices: agree, strongly agree, disagree, strongly disagree, or no answer. This Leikert scale (named for its creator) elicits more than a simple affirmation or dismissal—it brings out your emotion. Pollsters are looking for positive or negative views of such strength, that persons giving the answers will act on their beliefs.

The writer uses his or her strongly held beliefs, ideas, and points of view to produce powerful writing. To tap your strongest positions make two lists, side by side: things you love (strongly agree) and things you despise (strongly disagree). Choose the one that brings out your most powerful response. Write *fervently* about it today.

Transfusion

I think if painting and music as subcutaneous *arts. They get under your skin. They may get deeper than that eventually but it takes a while, and they get there to some extent tinged but not diluted by the conditions under which you say them or heard them.*

Writing on the other hand strikes me as intravenous. *As you sit there only a few inches from the printed page, the words you read go directly into the bloodstream and go into it at full strength. If there is poison in the words, you are poisoned, if there is nourishment, you are nourished, if there is beauty, you are made a little more beautiful.*

In Hebrew, the word dabar *means both word and also deed. A word doesn't merely say something; it does something. It brings something into being. It makes something happen.*

Frederick Buechner[1]

10

If you have ever lost blood and needed a transfusion, Buechner's analogy makes sense. Words on paper, even more than words spoken, are taken in straight, just the way the writer arranged them. The effect they have on you depends somewhat on your need for them. As with blood delivered right into the vein, words can fix a system gone awry. Words beget thoughts like plasma generates new blood cells.

We select the words to read that deliver what we need—all are not the same. A summer-read, a quick read, or a serious read give us different kinds of pleasure or insight at different times. Our system rejects words we find dull, pompous, confusing, or offensive, like a transplanted organ that does not match.

"No tears in the writer; no tears in the reader; no surprise for the writer, no surprise for the reader," said Robert Frost. The words we write, like the words we read, can make something happen in us, as well as in the reader. Part of the impetus for writing is to keep the blood coursing through the veins. "Lifeblood" speaks to the essential nature of blood. Writing may be essential to your life.

Poison Words

In the morning David wrote a letter to Joab and sent it with Uriah.

II Samuel 11:14

The unsuspecting Uriah delivered a letter with his own death orders from King David to Joab, the captain of the army. The letter was probably sealed with the king's ring imprinted on wax so the mail carrier could not read of his fate. Uriah was such a loyal soldier; he didn't even go home to his beautiful wife Bathsheba because the rest of the army and the ark were still exposed. David's scheme to cover his adultery, and the child conceived as a result, was foiled when Uriah put duty over home.

The letter Uriah carried was as direct as it was incriminating. Uriah must perish. After Joab accomplished the deed, a messenger hurried to David to deliver a verbal report with news of Uriah's death. David waited only long enough for Bathsheba to mourn and then sent for her to be his wife.

Then God sent his message to David in the person of Nathan, the prophet: an allegorical story, "Two men, one rich, one poor ..."

A letter, a verbal message, and a story—all ways of communicating the reality of evil. Bad news travels fast, it has been said. Now by cell phone and fax and e-mail it travels even faster. Voice mail and answering machines also require no human connection in order to deposit bad news.

Joab probably dropped the letter from David into the fire and camouflaged the death of Uriah into war news. But the story told by Nathan stuck like a burr in David's consciousness. Finally the tormented king admitted his sin.

I save letters—even those containing bad news. When I want to go back, a specific letter is hard to find. But my memory for story requires neither good filing or good news. Selective as it may be, my mind delivers ancient story messages from a mental circuitry, while I'm awake and even asleep. Nothing I've experienced in my life can disappear without a trace. So I give up on erasers, inkblots, fires, and the computer delete button as ways to destroy the past. I never know when a snippet from my memory bank will find its way onto the printed page. Confession, testimony, truth—all waiting to be told.

Dear God,

The mind is an amazing thing; I am in awe of its wireless capacity. Grant that I may use its powers for good. Amen.

Coworkers in Creation

The artist must be within his work like God within Creation; invisible and all-powerful; we feel him throughout, but we cannot see him.

Gustave Flaubert[2]

"All writing is autobiographical..." I've heard said. Even fiction reflects the world as seen, experienced, or imagined by the writer. The trouble comes when a reader tries to make a scene-by-scene correspondence to a life. The events or snippets of life are scrambled and then assembled in a different order—creating new from old.

In memoir, the author acknowledges that these things happened to her but uses them as a point of reflection. In Patricia Hampl's *I Could Tell You Stories*,[3] one brief scene of an unlikely, mismatched couple saying goodbye before the woman boards a bus became the basis for a treatise on memoir. The focal point moved from author to experience to curiosity, not about the observer, but about the significance of the observed.

Even the personal essay—so blatantly an "I" story—quickly diverts the reader's attention from writer first person to reader first person. The essayist says, in effect, come see or feel or sense with me so that it becomes your observation or understanding. If you find *you* in my words, you will forget the *I* who penned it. I choose to use "I" in these meditations for writers because I do not presume my readers have had the same experience or reaction to it, and only I claim the gospel according to me. Each reader will embrace the veracity of the words only if they jibe with her own past or future.

I'm realistic enough to know that only a few people who already know me will even care about me as a particular "I." A few readers may want to know me or look for other books I've written, but mostly they will regard me as a door opener or window blind raiser to creation. Through my quirky self, others may recognize our common humanity.

Phillip Lopate puts the problem of egotism into perspective in *The Art of the Personal Essay*: "The trick is to realize that one is not important, except insofar as one's example can serve to elucidate a more widespread human trait and make readers feel a little less lonely and freakish."[4] Personal essay invites other travelers to come along.

Dear God,

When I consider the moon and the stars … what is man that you are mindful of him? You have crowned us to be a light to ward off the darkness, for others and ourselves. Amen.

Mastering the Masters

You must lurk in libraries and climb the stacks like ladders to sniff books like perfumes and wear books like hats upon your crazy heads.

Ray Bradbury[5]

I've decided to get my master's of fine arts in writing. My teachers will be Annie Dillard, William Zinsser, St Augustine, Dan Taylor, Peter Elbow, Saint Paul, William Safford, and Rainer Marie Rilke. They and many more have agreed to come to my home for a private tutorial; sometimes they all want to talk at once. Many of my teachers insist I have to read their best works before they will tell me just how and why they wrote them. The tuition is as modest as the cost of a book.

Part of the reason I am writing this book is that my teachers insisted. It is not enough to read good literature or read about writing. If you are to master writing—write! Don't just think about it or talk to friends about that novel inside or search for the right place or time to write. Teachers give assignments. They expect to see the fruits of their shared wisdom become ripe in due time.

I like assignments and deadlines. They get me off my perch of indecision. The drawback of my school is that the teachers are lenient. If I don't follow their advice or emulate their style, there are no tangible consequences such as low grades, scorn, flunking out. If it were not for my own internal taskmaster and its ever-present, finger-pointing shame, I'd still be reading about writing.

An eighty-year-old woman whose memoirs were just published gave this advice: "Enter contests. They give you deadlines. You may even win." Sometimes I enroll in community writing courses of questionable value just to get assignments. Or I promise myself I'll write every day. Or I pick a theme for a group of meditations and decree I must produce one everyday before I may leave the desk.

Some writers are born into the profession. Others (I speculate most of us) have never enrolled in a master's program but have gone the cheaper route and are self-taught by the masters.

I'm a Calvinist with a conscience. About the time I want to chuck the whole writing enterprise, I'm reminded that I've been given this life work for a purpose. Use it or lose it to someone else, my best teacher says. I don't want to hear the words: "Take the talent from him and give it to the one who has the ten talents" (Matthew 25:28).

Dear God,

   Speak to me through your Word and the words of the great books. Amen.

Throwaway Words

Fix these words of mine in your hearts and minds; tie them as symbols on your hands, and bind them on your foreheads. Teach them to your children, talking about them when you sit at home and when you walk along the road, when you lie down and when you get up. Write them on the doorframes of your houses ...

Deuteronomy 11:18–20a

M any decry the Internet and its instant communication. Look at it this way: More people are writing more words than ever before. E-mail may be keeping us literate! Not that the quality of the words is always stellar, but they are words nonetheless. Words carry meaning. One can speculate, declare, propose, comment, encourage, and share with words. Record, review, remind, rebuke, reminisce, reinforce, reiterate, and render ideas, events, thoughts, and plans. But e-mail words are no more than throwaway words unless we press the print key and store the printed page. Some e-mail missives are not worth saving; others are as valuable as precious stones. I rarely throw away a letter that comes by the U.S. mail. They are nearly relics in their own time!

When I sense, after the first few sentences of an e-mail message, that I have a real one coming over the transom, I print and read it in black and white. I can make a value judgment at that point—keep or pitch. I like the fact that, when I set about to answer the communication, their letter to me is attached, giving me a handy record of letter out/letter in. Word-cause and word-effect. It has its advantages over writing alone to an unknown audience and getting only rare feedback.

Some of us banter words about in chat rooms or on a designated listserve. The list I was on for several years was intimidating. No one wrote "lightly." The shared pieces tended to be long and substantive. I rarely dared to contribute my lightweight ideas. If a topic was of interest, I printed the writing that spoke to me and advanced the argument of the thread starter. The mass communication "forwards," which I receive as one of a long list of recipients, I never read. More value judgments. Selective listening to words that might possibly be worth saving.

Words written but not worth saving scare me. What if my own words are good for nothing? That will be for others to decide. My job is to record, in whatever venue at my disposal, words that convey truth—my truth. Words offer those possibilities. But, I wonder, which words are important enough to carve above my front door?

Dear God,

You place a high value on words. Without them will we remember you? *Amen.*

Me, Myself, and I

I, Paul, write this greeting in my own hand, which is the distinguishing mark in all my letters. This is how I write.

II Thessalonians 3:17

Those who learned to write in the 1940s and 1950s in grade school knew it was a cardinal sin ever to use the first person "I" or "me" in an essay or a theme. Imagine writing "What I Did Last Summer" without one reference to yourself—the person who experienced it all. A student could always hide behind "we" or "my family," but so often the best parts of summer only happened to me, myself, or I.

The editorial "we" or the very formal reference to "the writer" made all writing seem like a news item or a secondhand report. Even as a feature writer for the high school newspaper, I had to keep my distance from anything experiential.

The arrival of the personal essay changed all that. Although the form dates back to Seneca, it has only recently been legitimized by people such as Phillip Lopate and raised to an art form. After years of writing very personally in my journal, my first attempts to "write something" for the eyes of others came out as personal essays. When I enrolled in a class by that name, it became clear that most writers not schooled in writing fell into the form naturally. As we read our work to each other, we discovered the writing that connects is often very personal. It is also full of detail of place and persons, creating a richness of setting and movement of story.

Things have changed in school. When my daughter was in second grade, she was already being encouraged to complete "I" stories for which her teacher supplied the first line. I have cherished them for twenty-five years. My granddaughter recently gave me a report she wrote on Australia. Her assignment was to write it as journal entries. What a way to elevate a dull report to a lively first-person adventure!

Now I read popular books, such as *Life of the Beloved* by Henri Nouwen and *Amazing Grace* by Kathleen Norris and realize they connect precisely because they are written in the first person. I become more than an anonymous reader. Novels with a first-person narrator, such as *Romey's Place* by James Schaap, are gaining popularity. The proliferation of memoir and autobiography shows how much readers enjoy real-life closeness.

Stories of faith are always personal.

Dear God,

Let me write as boldly as Saint Paul about what you have done in my life. Amen.

Misspellers Anonymous

I recall exactly where I was the day I heard about a computer program that could correct a writer's spelling. My son Doug and I were moving down a hallway with Jeff, the computer specialist at the rehab hospital, who encourages disabled persons to utilize the wonders of technology. Doug is unable to walk or use his hands because of a spinal cord injury, but he is not spelling disabled. He looked at me and spilled the truth, "My mom could use that."

"How does it work?" I asked Jeff, and he took me to the computer to demonstrate. I had visions of a little man inside the machine, hopping around with a red pencil, and marking up my paper. When I saw the cursor stop on a questionable word and offer me an alternative, I was transfixed. The idea of an electronic dictionary, against which my miserable words are compared, was incomprehensible. "It's a miracle" I squealed like a schoolgirl who had just seen the acne disappear from her face because of a new cream. I instantly saw that this wonder of technology would change my life. Jeff didn't know of my lifelong struggle; Doug understood enough to see the computer writing on the screen, as he said "Nothing can stop her now."

Today I am past embarrassment over my inability to spell, but it was the one factor that for a time held me back from becoming the writer I dreamed of being. Some days I think I know just a little of the struggle of persons with cerebral palsy, who have trouble communicating. To have thoughts trapped inside, with no way to get them out, seems the ultimate frustration. Just as the Bliss Board, a communication device for the language disabled, brought release to so many, spellcheck is doing the same for people like me. The numbers of us failed spellers are legion, I believe, if my experience is typical. When I publicly confess that I lack the spelling gene, others chime in, "I have the same problem!" I wonder how many of them have held back from their writing dreams out of sheer mortification that their failings will be smeared right across the page for all to see.

When I started graduate school in 1981, I had never used a computer. I learned on an Apple II and quickly tried all the gizmos for moving text and revising on the spot. The first paper I typed for a class was a breeze, but just as I was handing it in I noticed a spelling error. The manuscript was full of them. The day I met Jeff at the hospital I was well into my dissertation. My euphoria over spelling help for the project at hand quickly disappeared when I realized spellcheck was then only available on the Macintosh; and, of course, my word processing program was not yet transferable. So close, but not quite there.

I've given up trying to identify the cause of my disability. Didn't I get As in spelling in grade school? Couldn't I look at anyone else's writing and pick out the misspelled words? Didn't I want to spell correctly more than anything else in the world? If good spelling relied on desire, I would be the greatest.

My mother, the consummate speller, who even manually spell-checked my 250-page dissertation, thinks my problem is due to the way I was taught to read. Phonics was out of fashion when I learned to read; she thinks I suffered. And knowing more today, I believe I was dyslexic before the condition had a name. I was a slow, halting reader—something that has made learning even more precious all my life. Perhaps I just can't attend to detail, like all those letters arranged between the beginning and ending sounds of a word.

My family has been kind for the most part. While in college I wrote home frequently about my life of "studing." Finally my father, who was ever a harsh critic of oral pronunciation, gently corrected me. My professors must have liked me, but it was their job to teach, not be nice guys. No wonder I nearly flunked freshman English when my final paper contained more than twenty spelling errors.

Not long ago, before I began typing and using spellcheck on all my letters, my sister, who has no scholarly ambitions, had to remark that every one of my "lovely, long letters" (hey, butter me up) contained one or two spelling errors. I guess it became something of a parlor game in my family. I'm sure my voluminous journals will one day provide my ancestors many good laughs. The best speller I knew while growing up never went beyond high school. I guess some have the speller gene, and some don't. I imagine St Paul's "thorn in the flesh" to be the same as mine. It hurts constantly and cannot be willed away. For failed spellers like me, there should be a misspellers' anonymous. What would a twelve-step program for us look like?

Back in the 1970s I started a newsletter to promote a cause I believed in. It went out monthly. At first I had help, and someone regularly checked the contents before printing. But when the help dwindled, the spelling errors increased. Embarrassed, I gave up the editorship. Today, I teach an occasional workshop in grantwriting. I made a written syllabus (duly spell-checked) so I won't have to write on the board. When I do brainstorming sessions for work, I always find someone, like my high school friend, to be the recorder.

For better or worse, I have something to say, and my medium is not the spoken word but the written one. Any misspelled words are right there in black and white, distracting the reader from anything interesting I am trying to communicate. Those misplaced letters cast aspersions on me, unfairly perhaps, but they do, nonetheless. And despite my disability and all the pain it has caused me, I see the misspelled words of others and can't help wondering about them.

Years ago I jokingly told a brilliant workmate, who happened to be left-handed, that she should get someone else to sign her letters because her handwriting looked like a third grader's. Her instant reply was: "Get someone to correct your spelling 'cause you look like you've never been to school!" She was serious.

Years later we met and shared what we were doing with our lives. "I've started my own business as a technical writer," I stated with some pride. She laughed out loud, quickly covering her mouth, but not able to hide her honest reaction. My explanation was simple: spellcheck!

Today my son, who typed for years with two knuckles, and my husband, who forgot how to type once he had a secretary, use a voice-activated word-processing program that frees them to do their writing. They urge me to try it. "Thanks anyway," I smile, "I've got all the help I need." Documents, e-mail, poems, and essays spill off the printer daily. Now they can see the light of day—my fear is gone. Unless, of course, I fail to proofread for spellcheck errors.

Tips, Hints, and Advice

Don't write personal essays if you are nervous about your privacy. You must be a real person, not a caricature.

1. Words "do" something, according to Buechner. Some writers do not care what their words do to the reader; most do not plan for a specific effect. When we critique a piece of writing with the question, How did it make you feel? we are gathering a "doing" barometer. I know folks who refuse to read or watch a story that does not have a happy ending. If the ending is inconclusive or downright sad, they feel tricked, as if "all lived happily ever after" were a requirement. Nonfiction, like this book, does not create story—it tells real stories or gives real advice or real encouragement. Nonfiction can do something *practical* but, for lasting value it must also do something *emotional*. Better yet, it can do something *spiritual*.

2. In the aftermath of Gulf War II, looting was rampant in Iraq. One story struck me. Every thing, down to the fuses, was taken from the lavish home of a Baath party executive. Only papers remained, strewn about and trampled. Only words were worthless to looters. Those disheveled papers, however, revealed more about the home's inhabitant than all that was confiscated. If you want to remain anonymous when political tides turn, don't leave your papers behind.

3. The first book I read specifically about the personal essay was by Sheila Bender.[6] The author presented eight types of personal essays, illustrating them with writings. My teacher assigned an essay of one type each week. The discipline of conforming to instructions stretched me to write on topics and in ways that previously had not come naturally. The next Christmas I assembled the essays in a booklet as a gift for my family. The

booklet was my debut, a maiden voyage into publishing. I didn't get much feedback, which was probably just a well. It was hard enough to let go of my precious words and go public. But seeing my writing between covers increased my sense of purpose. I've been making little books ever since.

4. Books "about writing" dominate my library. I am almost always reading one along with a book for pure pleasure. I have read more advice about the craft of writing than I can ever use. In addition, I collect books of essays and memoirs. When an author makes an impression, I search for other works he or she has published. In writing the hints for new writers in this book, I searched my memory, not the books on my shelf. Only those prompts that I actually used and assimilated are recorded here. Only the lingering voices of essayists find their way into my consciousness. All messages will not speak to you. Choose carefully; discard the chaff that won't work. Bundle up the good seed and plant it, each time you write.

5. Writers need periodic transfusions when their writing passion wanes. Seasoned writers try various techniques during writing sessions, like taking a walk or a run or a power nap. Anything to get the pen out of hand for a short while. The writing goes mental, either consciously or subconsciously. If the slump last longer due to illness or disillusionment with a project or repeated rejection of their work, larger solutions are needed.

6. Living between thirty and forty-five minutes away from our three children and their families has been a good buffer for me. They don't ask (or if they do, I decline) me to care for the children for an hour at midday. If my home were down the block, refusing would be more difficult. Instead, I offer when I am in town to give them an hour or two for a quick getaway. But mainly I offer the occasional substantial break—a weekend or a week of having the kids here. I find it easier to let go of work and major in children. What concessions do you make to leave your desk? Is it possible to "make up" for lost or repurposed time? Is your diversion one that can add to your storehouse of writing material, to be held in abeyance until quiet is restored? I hate to be pulled from my desk, but often it benefits my writing and me.

7. One man in our workshop told of a novel approach to getting writing done. This busy Episcopal priest put his writing aside in the press of ministry. The homily constituted his written output for the week. One of his parishioners, after reading his story of a deathbed visit, offered to become his writing coach. She admitted she didn't know much about the mechanics of writing except for her own love of a good story. So they made a plan. Every Saturday morning she'd stop by his house to pick up a fresh piece of writing. She would accept no excuses. Not wanting to disappoint her and break their agreement, he met the deadline even if it meant a late-night session or an early morning rise. Sometimes they would talk, but mostly she simply took the essay, read it, and returned it the next week with

some general reader comments. She served a coach's capacity: encouragement, schedule, tapping natural talent, and showing up ready to play. Would your output increase if you had such a coach? Find one.

8. Even though the individual "I" in a personal essay must give way to the inclusive "I" of the reader, that person (you or the first person narrator of the story) must be one a reader cares about. Without the reader's identifying with a real or believable person, his outcome matters little. Don't write personal essays if you are nervous about your privacy. You must be a real person, not a caricature. If you make yourself sound too good to be true, the reader will look elsewhere for someone closer to his experience. Someone real.

9. I have trouble writing long essays. At about 1,000 words I get weary and imagine the reader tiring, too. So I go into my "find an exit" mode and try to escape. I want to get done with the story. To ease my departure, I move from specific detail to generalizations and proclamations. Yet "Stay in the moment," is what my teachers entreat. "Tread water and look around." What is really happening here? Is there a reason I can't get close to this? Can I show it instead of telling it? If done well, the added words will enhance the story, giving the reader a view right into your head. You won't have to explain anything. Be patient with your story and it will get told.

Writing Challenge

10

Write a story about yourself as a writer.

Technology changed my life. Without being too melodramatic, I confess that my spelling disability nearly prevented my access to the world of writing. Shame, embarrassment, and second-guessing erected barriers so tall that I could not get over them. The essay in this chapter tells my story. Your experience may be quite different. However, most of us are second- or third-career writers. We missed those wonderful early epiphanies that great writers tell of at the age of five or ten. We always knew we wouldn't be writers.

Spellcheck was invented in my lifetime, as were computers and laser printers and the Internet. They have combined to be just the adaptive devices I needed to finally dare to get my thoughts on paper.

What barriers did you have to overcome to get to this place? Write a story or poem or an essay about yourself as writer. Even using that word "writer" to describe yourself may lead to a whole new self-concept. Enjoy it; own it.

Creation

In the Genesis account we read that God created human beings in his own image and entrusted them with the task of carrying on the activity of creation, giving further form to the raw material of nature, actualizing the potentials tucked away in the world in a way which serves human society and at the same time glorifies God and his lavish benevolence. When we carry out this project in our own work we do something godlike.

Lee Hardy[1]

11

"Giving form to the raw material of nature,"—*that's it!* That's what this writing business is all about! It's easy to think of materials as raw when their most common refined form is as a useful object. When a line storm took down many mature, sturdy trees in our woods, my husband contracted with a man with a portable saw mill. The sections of logs became boards; the boards are becoming beds and tables and trim. The wood might have rotted on the ground, feeding the forest, but it was repurposed.

Artist Ray Materson discovered his creativity in prison where he fashioned an embroidery hoop from a plastic bowl and unraveled socks for floss. *Sins and Needles* tells his story of the beginnings of creative expression under the most difficult of circumstances. Materson says, "Just as sure as people are born to create, I believe that if their talents and gifts aren't encouraged, they become destructive. Sometimes they destroy others, but more often, they destroy themselves."[2]

We are limited creators; we cannot make something out of nothing. But our God-likeness allows us to gather raw materials and form new entities. Creativity has been described as combining two unlike things to form something new. Inventors, visual artists, teachers, and mimes all work with a medium they understand and use it to approach something they do not know. A writing teacher once asked his students to pick two words out of a revolving barrel and, by writing, force the random words into a relationship. A new creation emerged. Writing is god-like work.

May the favor of the Lord our God rest upon us; establish the work of our hands for us—yes, establish the work of our hands.

Psalm 90:17

Come, Holy Spirit

This is what we speak, not in words taught us by human wisdom but in words taught by the Spirit, expressing spiritual truths in spiritual words.

I Corinthians 2:13

Many writers report that when thoughts are rapidly flowing from head to paper, they enter a state where nothing else matters. And even as the pen moves, the writer seems to be *watching* rather than *doing* the work. Novelists sometimes blame their fictional characters who, they imagine, take on a life of their own, leaving the writer as a mere recorder. My rational mind would like to explain the phenomenon away, but when I read a finished piece of work, I am amazed that the words recorded really came from me. I read them as if for the first time!

Talking with Christian friends, Jean and Dale, whom we are visiting in Arizona, I try to explain what sometimes happens to me when I write. It is as if the Spirit of God comes over me and fills me so that words just tumble out. This happens even when I write an essay without a particular spiritual emphasis. I'm almost embarrassed to claim inspiration—knowing how much religious baggage that carries.

The next night Jean invites a friend to join us for dinner because he shares an interest in biological science with our husbands, both retired professors. The scientists talk about the serendipity of scientific discoveries with the same sort of wonder I feel after writing something surprisingly good. Jean, never one to pass an opportunity to tell others of her faith, blurts out, "It is the same thing that happens to Carol when she writes. It's God's Spirit that makes sense out of chaos—supplying everything we need."

The message might have surprised the guest, but to the rest of us it was clear: "God moves in mysterious ways, his wonders to perform." How he moves will always be a mystery. And for that matter, we ask, why does God choose to use both believers and unbelievers to be his creators and word-bearers? But, as Christians, we know the power from personal experience, and we know the source.

Madeleine L'Engle has put it beautifully: "An artist is a nourisher and a creator who knows that during the act of creation there is collaboration. We do not create alone."[3]

Dear God,

Thanks for your Spirit—your living presence that constantly amazes me as I work. Come, kindle a flame within me. Make yourself known to all writers. Amen.

A Terrible Thing

Let the word of Christ dwell in you richly as you teach and admonish one another with all wisdom … with gratitude in your hearts to God.

Colossians 3:16

It's a terrible thing to say no to God!" concluded the young woman. The audience laughed and then applauded as she left the podium. The quote ended a story of her grandfather's opposition to her studying theology to become a preacher. Grandpa and many of his generation believed that God ordained for all time that preaching was for men only.

But his granddaughter could talk the language of faith. "Do you believe that God called you to be a farmer?" she asked with a twinkle in her eye. "Yes, I do," he said with confidence. "How did you know?" was her next question. "Well, he didn't actually say 'John, I want you to raise corn,' but he gave me talents and put opportunities in my path. Then, as I began, he blessed my efforts and made me feel proud to be a farmer."

"Grandpa, God gave me a love of his Word and a desire to share it with others. Remember how I loved to go to church when I was just a little girl and even listened carefully to sermons? One day God convinced me that I should preach, too. I tried to present a substitute, but none would do. It's a terrible thing to say 'No' to God!" What could Grandpa say?

I was in the audience, but I did not laugh. I had done that terrible thing. When I was young, I was convinced God called me, too. He gave me a heart for the church, and while still in high school I found myself eager to attend the regional governance meeting in which a candidate for the ministry was being "examined." I was moved and thrilled and challenged—by God. But for all sorts of good reasons, I said "No." The church rules, my Dutch community, the seminary all said "No," and at seventeen, I was not bold enough to buck the system. But even at thirty and forty, as I fought the powers that preserved the status quo for women, I was still not bold enough to become a preacher.

Last week, I attended the graduation from a theological seminary of my friend Kathy. What a thrilling day! She said, "Yes," and God blessed her. Times have changed. Although some of the institutional barriers have been removed for women, still it has not been easy for her. But she will preach the Word.

That day, I admitted my private pain at saying "No." It *is* a terrible thing.

Dear God,

Forgive me for turning down your first call. Thanks for loving me still and gifting me for other work in your kingdom. Amen.

Subject: Grace

From the fullness of his grace, we have all received one blessing after another.
John 1:16

In the conclusion of his book, *What's so Amazing about Grace?*, Philip Yancey relates a story from the documentary movie by Bill Moyer entitled *Amazing Grace*. The scene is London's Wembley Stadium, at a musical celebration of racial changes in South Africa. The music is raucous rock, but the final performer is to be opera singer Jessye Norman. Her offering was "Amazing Grace"—written by John Newton, a slave trader turned preacher—which may have originated as a slave lament. Jessye Norman came on stage to boos from a revved-up crowd demanding more "rock." She began to sing anyway, without accompaniment, and a hush came over the crowd.

Yancey concludes: "… several thousand fans are singing along, digging far back in nearly lost memories for words they heard long ago."[4]

When we've been there ten thousand years,
Bright shining as the sun,
We've no less days to sing God's praise
Than when we'd first begun.[5]

"Jessye Norman later confessed she had no idea what power descended on Wembley Stadium that night. I think I know. The world thirsts for grace. When grace descends, the world falls silent before it."

God's Spirit came down not just upon this celebratory crowd, but much earlier on the men and women who had tried to preserve apartheid as a way of life. People, who once believed that God's Word actually mandated the separation of the races, now could see the system as evil, destructive, and hope-robbing.

The Spirit of God infiltrates all of life—delivering grace where it is unwanted and, of course, undeserved. The presence of the Spirit can rescue a faulty human gift for use in the kingdom. In the act of writing, the person and the product are both transformed by God's mysterious power. The Spirit stills a troubled mind or an anxious heart, freeing the author to write from a depth unknown to her, producing words and thoughts that sometimes come as a surprise. Oh, the grace of clarity of thought, direction, purpose. Truly amazing.

Dear God,

I am always surprised by your uncommon acts of kindness. Keep me from the haughtiness of thinking I deserved it. Amen.

Rising with the Sun

God came ... His glory covered the heavens and his praise filled the earth.
His splendor was like the sunrise; rays flashed from his hand, where his power was
hidden.

Habakkuk 3:3,4

If I could predict beautiful sunrises, I wouldn't have to keep a morning vigil in my dark kitchen. Weather people are no help. The things they can predict, like temperature and precipitation and even the time of sunrise or sunset, don't solve this problem. I want to know if the conditions are right for color in the sky. If they could warn me of upcoming beauty, as they do with meteor showers, I'd be in my ringside seat.

My husband thinks it a bit strange to see me sitting optimistic in the dark kitchen, my chair facing the window. He enjoys waiting less than I, especially when there is a chance the parade will pass us by.

There are a few clues as I walk the dog in the predawn light. Clouds are a good sign this morning, a week after winter solstice. The sun will be late, but the flattened egg of a moon still glows. The air feels crisp, clear. I begin to hope while brewing a cup of tea and taking up my observation post at the large window facing east. The finches, both scarlet and mustard yellow, amuse me while I look over the lake, through bare trees, and begin to see a tinge of pink on the underside of clouds. Without fanfare, the color above where the sun will be spreads until every cloud ripples richly, and an invisible brush coats others in both directions. Glorious color everywhere. As pink melts into orange, I know this morning's show is almost over.

If I could predict when my writing muse was likely to appear, I could set a date and be there expectantly. No waiting around. No wasting time. We'd be punctual and productive.

Before I became a writer, I read with horror about persons rising at five in the morning, long before today's eight o'clock sunrise, bundling in sweaters and wool socks, and trudging with coffee in hand upstairs for a morning write. All that before the real work of the day began. I knew it would take a miracle for me habitually to leave my warm bed hours before I had to. Sunrises and inspiration come at their own time. But if I am not there, I'll miss them totally. So I go regularly, albeit *after* dawn, to the desk and wait, now with my back to the window and every sense focused on the blank page. Some days I sit alone. No spark of color or form appears. But I'm still there, expectantly ready for beauty to happen.

Dear God,
   I boldly pray for beauty outside and within. Amen.

Longing for Home

I remember the days of long ago; I meditate on all your works and consider what your hands have done.

Psalm 143:5

We are in a rut. For more than forty years we have come back to the same old place in the Colorado Rockies, often more than once a year. My husband and I have traveled to other parts of the world with pleasure, but our hearts yearn to be right here in a remote log cabin in the Crystal River Valley. Part of the draw is beauty: Dramatic mountains rising from a valley cut by a crystal clear river; dry, clear air, perfect for wildlife discovery or star-gazing; the bluest skies and the whitest clouds. But the greatest pull is familiarity, the peace of home.

My fascination for the familiar drives me to see more and more in one place. While I despair of remembering the names of the hundreds of native flowers, their beauty is ingrained within me, even if I never get to Lead King Basin again. Longing and love keep bringing me back.

When I was eighteen, I wrote my first semblance of a poem while sitting beside the Carbonate Creek. I wonder how many others have been moved to write in this valley. Marjorie Franco said, "New writers are often told 'Write what you know.' I would broaden that by saying, write what you know emotionally."[6]

A robin decided to nest on the cabin's porch rafters this year, only a few yards from our slamming back door. Last week our household numbered ten, but Ms. Robin wasn't daunted by our hubbub. Her babies grew until the nest looked like an overcrowded tenement room. Mom will soon give them a push out on their own. Their wings could take them anywhere, but they will likely return nearby to raise their own young one day. Dozens of hummingbirds vie for sugar water in our feeder in midsummer, homing in on anything red. I can watch their frantic movements from a foot away, as long as I don't wear their favorite color or move even an eyelash. They must have scouts, because every time we are here, so are they.

The birds and the wildflowers and I share the imprint of this place. My parents brought me here when I was fourteen. My children now bring their children. We usually live far away from this "home," but the rut is deep. I close my eyes anytime, anywhere, and can see every turn of the Marble Road, the bouncing Crystal River, the mountain contours, the white blocks of marble sparkling in the sun. Even the history of this once bustling quarrying town is as alive as my own.

Write what you know, the teachers say. Marble, Colorado—you I know and love deeply.

Dear God,

You created us with a longing for home. Thank you for the gift of knowing with our hearts. Amen.

A Forced Relationship

And God saw that it was good. God blessed them and said, 'Be fruitful ...'
Genesis 1:21b, 22a

Acommonplace book[7] is a type of journal with a long literary tradition. William Gass refers to its use by Ben Jonson in *Defense of the Book*. The Commonplace Book is a repository for pleasing passages from the writings of others. The act of selecting and transcribing in one's own hand also sets the words "in the memory of the mind," says Gass.[8] Ben Jonson eventually reflected on the meaning of his entries and wove them seamlessly into his own writing.

A writing teacher in a continuing education class took the commonplace book idea a step further. He asked us to place our collected quotes on the upper and lower half of both sides of a looseleaf notebook page. Then we were to insert them in a notebook and cut each page in half. Because each half sheet moved independently of the others, any opening of the book revealed six possible combinations, up, down, across, and diagonal.

I've heard creativity defined as bringing two unlike things together to form an entirely new, third entity. The split book forced me to consider ways that two disparate passages might be related or might illumine each other. The same teacher had a rotating Plexiglas container filled with words on small pieces of paper. Once he told us to pick a word and write an essay around it (mine was *venison*!). Another day we picked two words with which to force a relationship and create a piece of writing.

"There is nothing new under the sun," the preacher says in Ecclesiastes (v. 1:9b). But there are infinite possibilities to combine the old and come out with something fresh. God places all the raw materials at our disposal and expects us to make a collage. This is the closest we writers will ever get to creation, but the exhilaration of making "a piece" may let us share some of the Creator's joy. Often I am embarrassed to stand back from a day's work and declare it "good." But perhaps, one day, God will give me the grace to survey my own work and give it a thumb's up.

Dear Creator,

You have given artists and scientists and builders everything they need. May we be fruitful and make beautiful combinations for you. Amen.

The Journey

"Do you journal?" ask my friends when they know I spend a lot of time writing. What an odd question. When did the noun *journal* become a verb, full of action and life? My old Webster's and my computer spellcheck do not acknowledge *journal* or *journaling* as verbs (here comes the red curvy line), and neither do many grammarians. But the act of frequently going to my little bound, blank book to write is the action verb I claim as a writer. For me, journaling came to life about twenty years ago, when writing became as physically and spiritually active as my passion for running had the decade before.

It took me two years of doodling during hard times to become the confirmed journaler I am today. Before a sudden bout of internal bleeding that almost took my life, the closest thing I did to journaling was keeping field notes on contacts with young blind children. Even though the notes were required for my job, I enjoyed reflecting on each day's encounters before the next day arrived.

The two months I spent in the hospital, mostly flat in bed, left me weak and discouraged. Once home, I sat at the dining room table after the family was off to work and school, staring blankly over the colorful backyard woods. Maybe I could read. Peter Elbow's *Writing Without Teachers* caught my eye. I borrowed some of my kid's notebook paper and gave freewriting a try. Without my usual energy, depleted after months of inactivity, I could hardly move the pen along the blank paper. Just ten minutes, Peter said—even that was a test of endurance. My mind was as sluggish as my hand. But the little sheaf of paper, which I still have today, testifies to progress toward wellness. Later, when the real activity of work and running was possible once again, I abandoned my fledgling journal.

I didn't feel the need to write again until a day in midsummer two years after my illness, when a water skiing accident left my seventeen-year-old son paralyzed. Hospital waiting, fear, tension, and boredom: I fought these then by writing in a small spiral notebook. Incredible sadness mixed with tiny spikes of hope found their way into that writing book. If it were not for those jottings, the year of his hospitalization would be no clearer than mist.

But *journal* did not become a verb until six months later when I went to help Mom sort through Dad's things after his sudden death. There on the shelf above his desk was a row of black daybooks. Inside one cover I learned where they came from: Woolworth's. Inspired by Dad's memory and the memoir he left the family, I searched the five-and-ten-cent store for a 1982 book like his. For the next ten years those identical daybooks gathered all the stuff I chose to pour inside. At times these books resemble a "Commonplace Book" full of wisdom from other writers or a prayer journal or a haphazard litany of pain. I count it as God's grace that the simple act of writing helped me accept the inevitable losses in my life.

When Woolworth's stopped printing daybooks, I graduated to larger bound books without dates and began to write only when moved to do so, which is often. Now, near-panic sets in when I realize the book is nearly filled and there is no blank journal waiting. Why this deep need to journal, now that I work daily at my writing? When I was a runner, I missed the endorphin high if too many days passed between long treks on the open road. Now that *journaling* has become as active as running for me, I have no choice. The journal is the open road. In its pages I have become the writer-in-training. Or perhaps, just the writer *being*.

**Tips,
Hints,
and
Advice**

*What does
it mean to be
a Christian
writer?
Writers
who are
Christian live
a powerful
message that
infuses their
writing.*

1. Why do kids like to be read to long after they can read for themselves? There is music in words well written. When that music comes from the voice of your mom or your friend or your spouse, the beauty multiplies. Enlarge the charm of your writing by reading it aloud, first to yourself and then to another. Oral reading reveals flaws in rhythm that can be easily corrected. Read your first draft aloud before putting it away. Does it sing? Or does it stutter? Fix it.

2. Not until I finished this collection and gave it to friends to read did I realize how predominantly my father is featured herein. One reader even suggested I call it *Words from My Father* referring both to God the Father and my own father. Dad died only six months after my son had a serious accident and was still in the hospital. In retrospect, I realize I was too preoccupied grieving my son's losses to grieve the loss of my father. For twenty years, thoughts of Dad continued to return, often stopping me at inconvenient times and demanding attention. His death was too sudden and not well timed, as death frequently is. Many important things were left unsaid between us. Sometimes they haunt me, so I write about them. Do you have some unfinished business you should attend to in your writing? Whether in a journal for your eyes only or writing to share with others who are in a similar place, letting the grief and remorse out on paper will clarify your feelings and may even heal you. What memories will not let you rest?

3. Long ago, in another season of my life, I taught preschool. My legacy from those years is a run-

ning tape in my head of songs and rhymes that young children love. When I'm with my small grandchildren, the songs and finger plays become part of our good times together. The ditties are not big on message, but they communicate exuberant fun. "I love you a bushel and a peck, a bushel and a peck and a hug around the neck ..." is as popular as "Jesus Loves Me." Sometimes, with the older children, I manage to infuse our good times with writing. This year some of them wrote or dictated stories for the annual Christmas giftbook. Writing that finds a place will live on. Make a place for your writing. Begin to create your own "Commonplace Book."

4. Technical writing is very appealing because of its rules. Form is prescribed depending on the journal, the information needed on an application, or the material expected on a proposal. I used to chat with professors who publish frequently about how they write. Most journals, especially in science, allow for no flare in writing style. Facts drive the unembellished words. Form rules; conformity is essential. Not so for creative writing. Form cannot be superimposed upon the work, but must emerge from it in a more organic way. An essay without form rambles. Perhaps form will not be discovered until all the words are written. Finding form is as creative a process as is finding words.

5. I love the story of Genesis 1 when God looked over the dark universe and saw it as "formless and empty." All the raw materials were there, but they made no sense. Then God gave the universe form. God sorted some of the chaos during that

first week but some of the mess the Almighty left for men and women, the image-bearers of God. The notion that all the raw materials were created for our sorting should inspire writers. When I hear a particularly good talk by a writer and then rush out to buy her books, the reason is often her ability to sort ideas and articulate them well. That same Spirit of God, who "hovered over the waters," sometimes lingers around my desk as I seek to make sense of some part of my experience. Our job as cocreators is limited by the materials at hand. In God's vast creation, that is no limit at all.

6. Are there subjects that Christians should not write about? Since God created all things, all things fill us with wonder and curiosity. Some publishers and booksellers do not agree. They do not want to upset the sensibilities of other Christians with concerns or topics they would rather not face, such as offspring who are gay, personal greed, or addiction. However, evil exists. If writers do not face topics squarely, they may be covering their eyes and refusing to look out. Some Bible stories are not pretty, but they are all important. I want to learn about perplexing issues from people I trust who have firsthand knowledge. Christians can go a long way to meet this need, if they have the freedom to write about the things they know, as they struggle to understand their place in God's world.

7. What does it mean to be a Christian writer? I have avoided the use of that label because it categorizes the writer and creates prescribed expectations. Are you writing only for others in

your pew? The "Good News" is wide enough for those who have yet to find faith. Writers who are Christian live a powerful message that infuses their writing. The discerning reader will "know we are Christians" by the love we share.

Writing Challenge

11

Make at least five spiral-bound copies of your work and give them to friends and family. You are now a published author.

Now it's time for a new challenge. If you have followed the directives of the last ten chapters, you now have ten pieces of writing. After you reread them, decide if any of them have something in common and could cluster into a group. Arrange them in some order, either by subject or preference of topic—placing the ones you like best at the beginning and end of the pile. If you have not named each essay or poem, create one.

Now make a table of contents and give a name to the entire collection. When you have the name chosen, make a title page and put your name under it. You are on your way to publication!

But there is more hard work to do—revision! On the first rereading, think about the theme or the point of the writing. It may not be the one you set out to write and it may not resemble the assignment as you first understood it. Good! Those were just writing prompts; what you made of them is totally original.

Now, read over your work and make sure that every word and phrase somehow contributes to the theme. Cut the rest. Add some new words that reinforce the point. This will tighten your writing. If you have identified or been told about other trouble spots in your writing (like passive voice or weak verbs), reread the piece once with each problem in mind.

When you think you have reconsidered the writing carefully, read it once more aloud, either to yourself or to another person. As you read, you will usually spot mistakes such as awkward sentences or words that do not flow.

Now bring your camera-ready copy or a disk to a copy center. Make at least five, spiral-bound copies and give them to friends or family. Don't expect too much feedback. This exercise is for you, not them. You have gone public; you are a published author. You have caught the challenge. Now don't stop.

Epilogue

Over the years, my family and I have taken many a backpacking trip in the high country of Colorado. After several days of planning and acclimating to the altitude we load our packs and start up the trail, heading toward the first pass. Going up can be hard, especially while adjusting to the weight of the pack and the slope of the ascent. Occasionally an alpine meadow offers relief from climbing, and we catch our breath and glance upward and outward instead of just at our feet. We stop for breaks and, later, when we have gone the planned miles, set up camp for the night.

Unlike mountain climbers who go for the peaks, we packers go for the lowest high spot to cross before the descent. We revel in the views when we attain places such as Buckskin Pass. And as we climb we tell ourselves that we're doing the hard part—and that going down will be easier. But that is not always the case. On the way down breathing is certainly easier, but we use different muscles. Our calves tighten and heel blisters form. Steep places are slippery after rain or gravelly in the heat. But the hardest part is calculating on your downward hike how much energy the next ascent will require. The farther down one goes, the higher looms the next ridge, and the hiker must find new resolve to climb back up to the next pass.

"This is not fun!" declares one of the children during a particularly grueling hike. We listen and silently agree but continue to urge the whole group up the trail. Sometimes it means lightening a load or offering a treat of trail mix at the next rest stop. Or reminding them how magnificent the stars look at night when they are tucked into warm sleeping bags. Somehow each one has to find within him or herself what it takes to go on.

The writing life shares the same highs and lows. Exertion and exhilaration come in turns, helping to push even the reluctant writer onward. We imagine as we put one foot in front of the other that the view "from the top"—after the manuscript is completed, revised, submitted, and accepted—will be glorious. When exhaustion sets in and creativity ebbs, we are tempted to turn around, go back, without ever having tested ourselves and determined what we are capable of doing. But we do go on, and some experience the exhilaration of seeing our work in print. We may pause to admire the view, celebrate a little. But even then we know: We will return to the valley and, once again, make the climb.

Motivation is a mysterious phenomenon; creativity even more so. Each individual needs to find the will to continue to write. My goal in this book is to inspire and encourage you to press on, using words in ways that are incarnate with meaning. I hope you also find courage for the journey in Scripture, in the experiences with which you have been entrusted, from other writers, but most of all from feeling the presence of God's Spirit. In the valley, when God seems distant or absent, even your missing him can awaken the passion that renews your desire to write.

We don't know why God asks some of us to be his witnesses, especially to the stories of our lives. But God creates in me and in you the desire to write, and that desire is his call to action. If we say "yes" to the job of being a witness, we are promised, like Peter and the apostles: " ... the Holy Spirit, who is God's gift to those who obey him." (GN, Acts 5:32) Suddenly, the Spirit infuses us with uncommon fervor to tell about even the common events of life.

God not only brought all things into being, but he also upholds and nourishes all that exists. The food of a writer is less like a meal and more like a continuous transfusion, at least if she stays connected to the source. Then hopefulness replaces doubt; understanding overcomes limitations, and she finds the resolve to go forward in her labors. If William Safire is correct when he writes that " ... writing is less a profession than a professing ..." my hope is that through this book you will persist in giving witness to that which you have seen and believe.

God's call to write is not an order but an invitation. When I respond, God and I are in conversation—there is a real person on the other end of the line. I have a traveling companion. The road ahead may be unmarked and steep and confusing, but I am not walking alone. "Come," says the Spirit, "Come."

"Show me the way," I pray.

End Notes

Preface and Introduction

1. Susan Shaughnessy, *Walking on Alligators: A Book of Meditations for Writers.*
   (New York: HarperSanFrancisco, [Harper Collins]1993).
2. Anne Lamott, *Bird by Bird* (New York: Pantheon Books, 1994).
3. Frederick Buechner, *Now and Then: A Memoir of Vocation.*
   (New York: HarperCollins Publishers, Inc. 1983), 87.
4. Philip Yancey, *What's So Amazing About Grace.* (Grand Rapids, Mich.:
   Zondervan 1997).

Chapter 1

1. Madeleine L'Engle, *Walking on Water: Reflections on Faith and Art.* (Wheaton, Ill.:
   Harold Shaw Publishers, 1980), 25.
2. *Chimes.* Weekly student newspaper of Calvin College, Grand Rapids,
   Mich., 1933.
3. Peter DeVries, (1910–1993) known for books such as *The Blood of the Lamb*
   (Boston: Little, Brown and Co., 1961) and *Reuben, Reuben* (Boston: Little,
   Brown and Co., 1964).
4. Feike Feikema (pen name: Frederick Manfred) (1912–1994), known for books
   such as *Lord Grisly* (McGraw, 1954) and *The Primitive* (Doubleday, 1950).

Chapter 2

1. Madeleine L'Engle, *Walking on Water.*
2. *Dances with Wolves* (movie). Screenplay by Michael Blake, directed by
   Kevin Costner, Tig Productions (US), 1990.
3. *Anne Frank* (television miniseries, May 2001, American Broadcasting Company).
4. Andrew Sheehan, *Chasing the Hawk: Looking for My Father, Finding Myself.*
   (New York: Delacorte Press [Random House], 2001).
5. George Sheehan, *Running and Being: The Total Experience.* (New York: Simon
   and Schuster, 1978).
6. Kathleen Norris, *Dakota: A Spiritual Geography.* (New York: Ticknor
   and Fields, 1993).
7. Patricia Hampl, *A Romantic Education.* (Boston: Houghton Mifflin Co., 1981).
8. John Hockenberry, *Moving Violations: A Memoir.* (New York: Hyperion, 1995).
9. Nancy Mairs, *Waist-High in the World: Life among the Nondisabled.*
   (Boston: Beacon Press, 1996).
10. André Dubus, *Dancing after Hours.* (New York: Vintage Books, 1996).
11. Isaiah 38:12b, 19.
12. Lewis B. Smedes, *Forgive and Forget: Healing the Hurts We Don't Deserve.*
    (San Francisco: Harper & Row Publishers, 1984).

Chapter 3

1. Madeleine L'Engle, *Walking on Water*, 161.
2. Donald Hall, *Life Work*. (Boston: Beacon Press, 1993).
3. Anne Lamott, Lecture at Festival of Faith and Writing, Calvin College, 2000.
4. Louise DeSalvo, *Writing as a Way of Healing: How Telling Our Stories Transforms Our Lives*. (New York: HarperCollins Publishers, Inc., 1999).
5. William Safire and Leonard Safire, *Good Advice on Writing: Writers Past and Present on How to Write Well*. (New York: Simon & Schuster, 1992), 248.
6. C. S. Lewis, *Surprised by Joy*. (London: G. Bles, 1955).

Chapter 4

1. Phillip Lopate, *The Art of the Personal Essay: An Anthology from the Classical Era to the Present*. (New York: Anchor Books [Doubleday], 1994).
2. William Styron quoted in *Good Advice for Writers* by William Safire and Leonard Safire.
3. Paul Schrader, screenwriter, quoted in *Good Advice for Writers*.
4. Anne Beattie, from "Melancholy and the Muse," in *Unholy Ghost: Writers on Depression*. (New York: Morrow, 2001), 149.
5. Madeleine L'Engle, *A Circle of Quiet: Crosswicks Journal, Book I*. (New York: Farrar, Straus & Giroux, 1972).
6. Anne Lamott, continual challenges from *Bird by Bird*, (also *Traveling Mercies*, New York: Pantheon (Random House), 1999. *Operating Instructions*. New York: Fawcett Columbine, 1993.)
7. Michel de Montaigne (1533–1592) regarded as the father of the personal essay. *Michel de Montaigne: The Complete Essays* (translation by M.A. Screech). (London: Penguin Books, 1987).
8. John Jerome, *The Writing Trade: A Year in the Life*. (New York: Viking Penguin, 1992).

Chapter 5

1. Madeleine L'Engle, *Walking on Water*, 16.
2. Victor Frankel, *Man's Search for Meaning: An Introduction to Logo Therapy*. (Translator: Isle Lash, 1959) New York: Simon and Schuster, 1984.
3. Daniel 5:17, 5:22–28.
4. Song: "Come And Fill This Temple." Words and Music by Arlene Friesen.
5. Song: "Come Holy Spirit, Heavenly Dove." Words by Isaac Watts, 1707. Music by John B. Dykes, 1866. In hymnal for use in English Church by John Grey, 1866.

Chapter 6

1. Don Aslett and Carol Cartaino, *Get Organized, Get Published: 225 Ways to Make Time for Success*. (Cincinnati, Ohio: Writer's Digest Books, 2001).
2. Anne Lamott, in *Bird by Bird*.
3. Festival of Faith and Writing, a biennial writers' conference, Calvin College, Grand Rapids, Michigan, last held April, 2004. Dale Brown, Director.
4. Sally Stuart, *Christian Writers' Market Guide, 2004*. (Colorado Springs, Colo.: A Shaw Book [Waterbrook Press], 2004).

5. Madeleine L'Engle, *Walking on Water*, 34.
6. *Ora et labora* (Pray and work).
7. Annie Dillard, *Pilgrim at Tinker Creek*. (New York: Harper Perennial, 1998).
8. Barbara Brown Taylor, from lecture on April 24, 2004 at Festival of Faith and Writing, entitled "Way Beyond Belief: The Call to Behold."

Chapter 7

1. Frederick Buechner, *The Magnificent Defeat*. (New York: Seabury, 1966).
2. Text: p. 83, Matthew 5:6 (NIV).
3. Natalie Goldberg, *Wild Mind: Living the Writer's Life*. (New York: Bantam Books, 1990).
4. E. M. Forster, *Howard's End*. (New York: Penguin Books, 2000.)

Chapter 8

1. John Leax, *Grace is Where I Live: Writing as a Christian Vocation*. (Grand Rapids, Mich.: Baker Books, 1993), 27.
2. Thomas Merton, (1915–1968), American Catholic monk of the Trappist Order.
3. Baby Doe Regulations are based on 1984 amendment to the Child Abuse and Treatment Act, and require that, except in certain specified conditions, all newborns receive maximum life-prolonging treatment.
4. Joseph Epstein, "Early Rise: The Joy of Getting Out of Bed and Down to Work." *Atlantic Monthly*, Feb. 2002.
5. Phillip Lopate, *The Art of the Personal Essay*.
6. Rainer Marie Rilke, *Letters to a Young Poet*. (Novato, Calif.: New World Library, 2002).
7. Michel de Montaigne, *The Complete Essays*.
8. Patricia Clark, Associate Professor of English, Grand Valley State University.
9. John Leax, *Grace is Where I Live: Writing as a Christian Vocation*.
10. Tim O'Brien, *The Things They Carried: A Work of Fiction*. (Boston: Houghton Mifflin, 1990).
11. Donald Hall, *Life Work*.

Chapter 9

1. Suzanne Lipsett, *Surviving a Writer's Life*. (New York: HarperCollins Publishers, 1994).
2. Edna Ferber as quoted by William Safire and Leonard Safire in *Good Advice on Writing*.
3. Annie Dillard, *The Writing Life*. (New York: Quality Paperback Book Club,1989).
4. Mary Ann O'Roark, "How to Inspire," *Writer's Digest*, July 1999, 15.
5. Frederick Buechner, *The Hungering Dark*. (New York: HarperSanFrancisco [HarperCollins], 1969), 31.

Chapter 10

1. Frederick Buechner, *The Clown in the Belfry: Writings on Faith and Fiction*. (New York: HarperCollins, 1992), 76.
2. Gustave Flaubert, as quoted by William Safire and Leonard Safire in *Good Advice on Writing*.

3. Patricia Hampl, *I Could Tell You Stories: Sojourns in the Land of Memory*. (New York: W.W. Norton & Co., 1999).
4. Phillip Lopate, *The Art of the Personal Essay*.
5. Ray Bradbury, *Zen in the Art of Writing*. (Santa Barbara, Calif.: Joshua Odell Editions, 1966).
6. Sheila Bender, *Writing Personal Essays: How to Shape Your Life Experiences for the Page* (Cincinnati, Ohio: Writer's Digest Books, 1995).

Chapter 11

1. Lee Hardy, *The Fabric of This World: Inquiries into Calling, Career Choice and the Design of Human Work*. (Grand Rapids, Mich.: Eerdmans Publishing, 1990).
2. Ray and Melanie Materson, *Sins and Needles: A Story of Spiritual Mending*. (Chapel Hill, NC: Algonquin Books, 2002).
3. Madeleine L'Engle, *Walking on Water*.
4. Philip Yancey, *What's So Amazing About Grace?* (Grand Rapids, Mich.: Zondervan, 1997).
5. John Newton, song lyrics: "Amazing Grace." (Olney Hymns London: N. Oliver, 1779).
6. Marjorie Franco, quoted by William Safire and Leonard Safire in *Good Advice on Writing*.
7. Commonplace book: a bound volume in which aristocratic readers of the Renaissance would copy their favorite poems and quotes to which they would add their personal narrative. The practice illustrates the integrative nature of reading and writing.
8. William Gass, "Defense of the Book: Why Books are Good." *Harpers*, Nov. 1999.

Bibliography

Aslett, Don and Carol Cartaino. *Get Organized, Get Published: 225 Ways to Make Time for Success*. Cincinnati, Ohio: Writer's Digest Books, 2001.

Bender, Sheila. *Writing Personal Essays: How to Shape Your Life Experiences for the Page*. Cincinnati, Ohio: Writer's Digest Books, 1995.

Bradbury, Ray. *Zen and the Art of Writing*. Santa Barbara: Joshua Odell Editions, 1996.

Brown, W/Dale. *Of Fiction and Faith: Twelve American Writers Talk about Their Vision and Work*. Grand Rapids, Mich.: Eerdmans, 1997.

Buechner, Frederick. *Now and Then: A Memoir of Vocation*. San Francisco: HarperSanFrancisco (Harper Collins Publishers), 1983.

————. *The Magnificent Defeat*. New York: Seabury, 1966.

————. *The Hungering Dark*. San Francisco: HarperSanFrancisco (Harper Collins Publishers), 1969.

————. *The Clown in the Belfry: Writings on Faith and Fiction*. San Francisco: HarperSanFrancisco (Harper Collins Publishers), 1992.

————. *Listening to Your Life: Daily Meditations with Frederick Buechner*. (compiled by George Connor), San Francisco: HarperSanFrancisco (Harper Collins Publishers), 1992.

Carter, Jimmy. *An Hour before Daylight: Memories of a Rural Boyhood*. New York: Simon & Schuster, 2001.

————. *Always a Reckoning: And Other Poems*. New York: Crown Publishers, 1995.

Come And Fill This Temple, Song. Words and Music by Arlene Friesen.

Come Holy Spirit, Heavenly Dove, Song. Words by Isaac Watts, 1707. Music by John B. Dykes, 1866. In hymnal for use in English Church by John Grey, 1866.

Crafton, Barbara Cawthorne. *The Sewing Room: Uncommon Reflections on Life, Love and Work*. New York: Penguin Books, 1993.

de Montaigne, Michel. *The Complete Essays* (translated by M.A. Screech). London: Penguin Books, 1987.

DeSalvo, Louise. *Writing as a Way of Healing: How Telling Our Stories Transforms Our Lives*. New York: HarperCollins Publishers, 1999.

Dances with Wolves, Screenplay by Michael Blake, Directed by Kevin Costner, Tig Productions, 1990.

DeVries, Peter. *The Blood of the Lamb*. Boston: Little, Brown and Co., 1961.

————. *Reuben, Reuben*. Boston: Little, Brown and Co., 1964.

Dillard, Annie. *Pilgrim at Tinker Creek*. New York: Harper Perennial, 1998.

————. *The Writing Life*. New York: Harper & Row, 1989.

Dubus, André. *Dancing after Hours*. New York: Vintage Books, 1966.

Elbow, Peter. *Writing without Teachers*. Oxford: Oxford University Press, 1998.

Epstein, Joseph. "Early Rise: The Joy of Getting Out of Bed and Down to Work." *Atlantic Monthly*, February, 2002.

Forster, E.M. *Howard's End*. New York: Penguin Books, 2000.

Frankel, Viktor. *Man's Search for Meaning: An Introduction to Logo Therapy*. (Translater: Ilse Lash, 1959.) New York: Simon and Schuster, 1984.

Gass, William. "Defense of the Book: Why Books are Good." *Harpers*, Nov. 1999.

Goldberg, Natalie. *Wild Mind: Living the Writer's Life*. New York: Bantam Books, 1990.

_____. *Writing Down the Bones: Freeing the Writer Within*. Boston: Shambhala, 1986.

Hall, Donald. *Life Work*. Boston: Beacon Press, 1993.

Hampl, Patricia. *A Romantic Education*. Boston: Houghton Mifflin Co., 1981.

_____. *I Could Tell You Stories: Sojourns in the Land of Memory*. New York: W.W. Norton & Co., 1999.

_____. *Virgin Time: In Search of the Contemplative Life*. New York: Ballantine Books, 1992.

Hardy, Lee. *The Fabric of This World: Inquiries into Calling, Career Choice and the Design of Human Work*. Grand Rapids, Mich.: Eerdmans Publishing, 1990.

Hensley, Dennis. *How to Write What You Love*. Colorado Springs, Colo.: Shaw (Waterbrook), 2000.

Hockenberry, John. *Moving Violations: A Memoir*. New York: Hyperion, 1995.

Jerome, John. *The Writing Trade: A Year in the Life*. New York: Viking Penguin, 1992.

Lamott, Anne. *Bird by Bird: Some Instructions on Writing and Life*. New York: Pantheon Books, 1994.

_____. *Traveling Mercies*. New York: Pantheon Books, 1999.

_____. *Operating Instructions*. New York: Pantheon Books, 1993.

Leax, John. *Grace Is Where I Live: Writing as a Christian Vocation*. Grand Rapids, Mich.: Baker Books, 1993.

L'Engle, Madeleine. *Walking on Water: Reflections on Faith and Art*. Wheaton, Ill.: Harold Shaw Publishers, 1980.

_____. *A Circle of Quiet: Crosswicks Journal, Book I*. New York: Farrar, Straus & Giroux, 1972.

_____. *The Rock That Is Higher: Story as Truth*. Wheaton, Ill.: H. Shaw, 1993.

Lewis, C.S. *Surprised by Joy*. London: G. Bles, 1955.

Lindin, Roger. *Emily Dickinson and the Art of Belief*. Grand Rapids, Mich.: Eerdmans Publishing, 1998.

Lipsett, Susan. *Surviving a Writer's Life*. New York: HarperCollins Publishers, 1994.

Lopate, Phillip. *The Art of the Personal Essay: An Anthology from the Classical Era to the Present*. New York: Anchor Books (Doubleday), 1994.

Mairs, Nancy. *Waist-High in the World: A Life among the Nondisabled*. Boston: Beacon Press, 1994.

Materson, Ray and Melanie Materson. *Sins and Needles: A Story of Spiritual Mending*. Chapel Hill, NC: Algonquin Books of Chapel Hill, 2002.

McClanahan, Rebecca. *Write Your Heart Out: Exploring and Expressing What Matters to You*. Cincinnati, Ohio: Walking Stock Press, 2001.

Nelson, G. Lynn. *Writing and Being: Taking Back Our Lives through the Power of Language*. San Diego: LuraMedia, Inc., 1994.

Norris, Kathleen. *Dakota: A Spiritual Geography*. New York: Ticknor and Fields, 1993.

_____. *Amazing Grace: A Vocabulary of Faith*. New York: Riverhead Books (Penguin Putnam, Inc.), 1998.

Nouwen, Henri. *Life of the Beloved: Spiritual Living in a Secular World.* New York: Crossroad, 1993.

_____. *The Return of the Prodigal Son: A Story of Homecoming.* New York: Image Books (Doubleday), 1994.

O'Brien, Tim. *The Things They Carried: A Work of Fiction.* Boston: Houghton Mifflin Co., 1990.

O'Roark, Mary Ann. "How to Inspire." *Writer's Digest,* July 1999.

Rilke, Rainer Marie (Joan Burnham, translator). *Letters to a Young Poet.* Novato, Calif.: New World Library, 2002.

Safire, William and Leonard Safire. *Good Advice on Writing: Writers Past and Present on How to Write Well.* New York: Simon & Schuster, 1992.

Schaap, James. *Romey's Place.* Grand Rapids, Mich.: Baker Books, 1999.

Shaughnessey, Susan. *Walking on Alligators: A Book of Meditations for Writers.* San Francisco: HarperSanFrancisco (Harper Collins Publishers), 1993.

Sheehan, Andrew. *Chasing the Hawk: Looking for My Father, Finding Myself.* New York: Delacorte Press (Random House), 2001.

Sheehan, George. *Running and Being: The Total Experience.* New York: Simon and Schuster, 1978.

Smedes, Lewis B. *Forgive and Forget: Healing the Hurts We Don't Deserve.* San Francisco: Harper & Row, 1984.

Stafford, William. *Writing the Australian Crawl: Views on the Writer's Vocation.* Ann Arbor, Mich.: University of Michigan Press, 1978.

Stuart, Sally. *Christian Writers' Market Guide, 2004.* Colorado Springs, Colo.: Shaw (Waterbrook), 2004.

Taylor, Barbara Brown. *Home by Another Way.* Boston: Cowley Publications, 1999.

Taylor, Daniel. *Tell Me a Story: The Life-Shaping Power of Our Stories.* St. Paul, Minn.: Bog Walk Press, 2001.

_____. *Letters to My Children: A Father Passes on His Values.* Downers Grove, Ill.: InterVarsity Press, 1989.

_____. and Ronald Hoekstra. *Before Their Time: Lessons in Living from Those Born Too Soon.* Downers Grove, Ill.: InterVarsity Press, 2000.

Ueland, Brenda. *If You Want to Write: A Book about Art, Independence and Spirit.* St. Paul, Minn.: Graywolf Press, 1987.

Welty, Eudora. *One Writer's Beginnings.* Cambridge, Mass.: Harvard University Press, 1983.

Yancey, Philip. *What's So Amazing about Grace?* Grand Rapids, Mich.: Zondervan, 1997.

_____. and James Schaap. *More Than Words: Contemporary Writers on the Works That Shaped Them.* Grand Rapids, Mich.: Baker Books, 2002.

Zinsser, William, ed. *Inventing the Truth: The Art and Craft of Memoir.* Boston: Mariner Books (Houghton Mifflin Co.), 1998.

_____. *On Writing Well: The Classic Guide to Writing Nonfiction.* New York: Quill-A Harper Resource Book, 2001.

_____. *Writing About Your Life: A Journey into the Past.* New York: Marlowe & Company, 2004.

About the Author

After a long career in education and social service, Carol Rottman's desire to write led her into her own freelance writing business, which gave her the flexibility to spend more time writing for herself. Since then she has become an author and writing instructor who finds inspiration in everyday moments. "People seem to think that they need to live exceptional lives in order to be good writers. Some of my best writing has been inspired by simple incidents, such as being confined to the hospital for two months, or playing an intense game of Scrabble," says Carol. She says, however, that to become a good writer requires discipline, "When I began writing, I read every book about writing I could find, enrolled in classes, read the masters, and practiced every day."

In addition to *Writers in the Spirit*, Carol has published meditations in magazines and books such as *The Banner, These Days, My Heart I Offer*, and essays and articles in *The Banner, The Christian Communicator, Breaking Barriers, The Grand Rapids Press*, and *Cross and Quill*. In 2003 her essay, "Three Calls," received an award from *Writer's Digest*. She has taught numerous workshops and classes on writing, which include: "Journaling for Christians," "Telling Your Story on Paper: Creating Memoir," and "Writers in the Spirit."

Most recently, Carol was owner of First Draft Consulting, a writing service. She attended Calvin College for three years, then completed her undergraduate education at the University of Michigan, receiving a B.A. in elementary education in 1960. She went on to earn an M.A. in special education from Michigan State University and a Ph.D. in social welfare from Case Western Reserve University. After spending nineteen years as a teacher, primarily with infants and young children, she became director of the Research Agenda to Prevent Low Birth Weight, followed by six years as the manager of Perinatal Projects, for a health care organization in Cleveland. Throughout her career, Carol has been an active Christian lay-leader on denominational boards and church councils.

Carol and her husband Fritz have three children and eight grandchildren and live in rural Greenville, Michigan and Marble, Colorado. They make regular trips to Africa to help AIDS victims.